MW00332226

Powerful Parent Partnerships

It is essential that we work together to craft powerful parent-teacher partnerships that meet the needs of today's students and schools. In this important new book, authors Robert Dillon and Melissa Nixon show you how to build stable and supportive relationships with teachers so that the needs of your child are always met. They also offer strategies for staying involved in the school community at large. Loaded with practical takeaways and sample stories, this book will help you:

- Clearly communicate your child's educational goals;
- Make connections with other schools and school districts to build community and broaden your range of resources;
- Hold teachers and administrators accountable without alienating them;
- Develop communication strategies to address difficult topics like underperformance and misbehavior;
- Show compassion and gratitude;
- And more!

With the practical suggestions in this book, you'll be able to rekindle more engagement and excitement into your child's learning at school and at home.

Robert Dillon is an author, speaker, educator, and lifelong learner. His twenty plus years in education have seen him serve kids and families as a teacher, principal, technology director, and innovation leader. He has been honored by Common Sense Media, The Center for Green Schools, the dSchool at Stanford University, the Buck Institute for Education, and Future Ready Schools.

Melissa Nixon has served schools in central North Carolina for over 20 years as a teacher, assistant principal, principal, and as a district level administrator. Currently, she is a member of the International Board of Directors for Phi Delta Kappa and serves as an adjunct professor at High Point University in High Point, NC.

Also Available from Eye On Education

(www.routledge.com/eyeoneducation)

Education Write Now
Joe Mazza and Jeff Zoul

Passionate Learners:
How to Engage and Empower Your Students
Pernille Ripp

Intentional Innovation:
How to Guide Risk-Taking, Build Creative Capacity, and Lead Change
A.J. Juliani

Family Math Night K–5:
Common Core State Standards in Action
Jennifer Taylor-Cox

Family Math Night 6–8:
Common Core State Standards in Action
Jennifer Taylor-Cox

Family Reading Night, Second Edition
Darcy J. Hutchins, Joyce L. Epstein, and Marsha D. Greenfeld

Getting Parents on Board:
Partnering to Increase Math and Literacy Achievement, K–5
Alisa Hindin and Mary Mueller

School-Community Relations, Fourth Edition
Douglas J. Fiore

Empowering Families:
Practical Ways to Involve Parents in Boosting Literacy, Grades Pre-K–5
Judy Bradbury and Susan E. Busch

Multicultural Partnerships: Involve All Families
Darcy J. Hutchins, Marsha D. Greenfeld, Joyce L. Epstein, Mavis G. Sanders, Claudia Galindo

Powerful Parent Partnerships

Rethinking Family Engagement for Student Success

Robert Dillon and Melissa Nixon

Routledge
Taylor & Francis Group
NEW YORK AND LONDON

First published 2019
by Routledge
711 Third Avenue, New York, NY 10017

and by Routledge
2 Park Square, Milton Park, Abingdon, Oxon, OX14 4RN

Routledge is an imprint of the Taylor & Francis Group, an informa business

© 2019 Taylor & Francis

The right of Robert Dillon and Melissa Nixon to be identified as authors of this work has been asserted by them in accordance with sections 77 and 78 of the Copyright, Designs and Patents Act 1988.

All rights reserved. No part of this book may be reprinted or reproduced or utilised in any form or by any electronic, mechanical, or other means, now known or hereafter invented, including photocopying and recording, or in any information storage or retrieval system, without permission in writing from the publishers.

Trademark notice: Product or corporate names may be trademarks or registered trademarks, and are used only for identification and explanation without intent to infringe.

Library of Congress Cataloging-in-Publication Data
A catalog record for this title has been requested

ISBN: 978-0-8153-9444-0 (hbk)
ISBN: 978-0-8153-9445-7 (pbk)
ISBN: 978-1-351-18611-7 (ebk)

Typeset in Palatino
by Apex CoVantage, LLC

Contents

Meet the Authors

Robert Dillon is an author, speaker, educator, and lifelong learner. His twenty plus years in education has seen him serve kids and families as a teacher, principal, technology director, and innovation leader. His primary focus is working to bring synergy to instructional design, technology infusion, and learning space design. He believes that in this synergy is the educational gold that students need to be successful citizens in a modern world. He works through an equity lens and looks to bring excellence to every classroom. For this work, he has been honored by Common Sense Media, The Center for Green Schools, the dSchool at Stanford University, the Buck Institute for Education, and Future Ready Schools.

Melissa Nixon has been dedicated to her work in education for over 20 years. For this book, she draws upon her multiple perspectives of the educational system using her experiences as a classroom teacher, assistant principal, principal, and district-level administrator. Also, as a mother of two, her role as a parent provides further understanding of the need for Powerful Parent Partnerships. Her commitment to education is evident in her work as an adjunct professor at High Point University, North Carolina, where she builds knowledge for future school leaders about understanding diversity in education, school law and ethics, using data for school improvement, and 21st century leadership. She was elected to the Phi Delta Kappa International Board of Directors in 2015 and continues to serve the organization today. Dr. Nixon presents and has publications on Building Cultural Competency, Social Media for the 21st Century Educator, and Building Parent-Friendly Schools.

Preface

Having the dual role of being both a parent and an educator has likely been the most interconnected relationship in our lives. Hearing and seeing the wonder and curiosity of life through the eyes and ears of our children, only to watch that passion for knowledge slowly fade, has been an almost unbearable reality for us, especially when we know that amazing learning experiences are possible.

Innovation and creativity in the classroom require risk-taking and an understanding that our children are curious and inquisitive about life and the world. We want them to have experiences that make meaning and teach them to apply knowledge which will, in turn, help them navigate each day a little better than the one before. Instead, our current system does the very opposite; our schools open and close each day herding our children in like cattle, feeding their minds the same academic fodder that they did to the herd a year before only to be branded at the end of the year as "PROFICIENT."

Outside of the challenge of watching our children progress through the same series of corrals we did 25 years earlier, we are haunted by our desire to enact change but feel powerless at times to make it happen. We want our children to be a part of a system that is focused not only on making them "CAREER AND COLLEGE READY," but a system that focuses holistically on their social-emotional growth; for them to be part of a system that embraces emotional quotient (EQ) as much as intelligence quotient (IQ). We want their school work to be passion based and promote a deeper understanding. Most importantly, we want our children to apply their knowledge to the problems they encounter so that they can be the next generation of solution makers.

To make all of this a reality for all kids, it requires both schools and families working in rhythm with a new modern playbook. This book is designed to support those conversations, partnerships, and actions. Together educators and parents can craft a powerful partnership to meet these modern hopes and dreams for all children. This powerful partnership could begin with a list of principles that all involved (educators, students, and parents) could pursue together. Consider this list as a starting point.

We hope for:

- Schools that seek new ways to solve old problems;
- Schools that have teachers that like each other as people and spend time knowing each other's stories;
- Schools that have no boundaries; where life=school and school=life;
- Schools that seek answers instead of acting nice to parents;
- Schools that use communication to engage with the hard stuff as opposed to avoiding it;
- Schools that ask for forgiveness when they screw up;
- Schools that realize that their communities have assets and focus on bringing the community inside the school no matter the conditions in the community;
- Schools that reach out for partners. One county, one city, one district doesn't have the answers. It takes a cadre of solution makers to get it right.

Drs. Melissa Nixon and Robert Dillon

Introduction

As parents, caregivers, and families, we look deeply into the eyes of our children, and we see a longing to grow and learn, and, even though there are innovative things happening in most schools in the country, the role of being a parent in the modern school environment is more challenging than ever.

What can we do? How can we find advocates that are dedicated to making the learning the best it can be for all children? The joy of learning can be maximized, but it is going to take parents speaking up and asking for change in the right way. It is going to mean school communities believing that a new type of family involvement is foundational to success. It is going to mean communities surrounding schools.

Hearing and seeing the joy in children fade can feel like the ultimate failure of parenting and educating, and this book hopes to breathe life into the school/home relationship that has been eroding for many decades. The hope is to rekindle more engagement and excitement into more classrooms and help students love learning.

Having this deep passion for change is really difficult in a time and place when change happens so slowly in schools. It is becoming more and more obvious that schools struggle to be nimble and agile. It is hard for kids and families to understand that the speed of the world is accelerating, and many schools are more "horse and buggy" than ever before. This doesn't have to be reality. Schools, where parents and schools are looking for ways to co-support kids, are seeing real changes. These changes are coming from both conversations and actions.

With all of this said, we truly believe that teachers and leaders entered the profession with a desire to change lives. They want to make those in front of them and around them better. They want to support the growth of kids and families. There are so many roads forward, and so many examples of how excellence can flourish. There are incredible schools serving kids on a budget and with the rules and regulations, pensions and unions, and the need to serve the whole child in poverty coming through their doors. As parents, it is important that you know that there are real solutions, and we shouldn't rest until we are in deep partnership with the school to make that a reality. As a parent, we have a choice about the type of parent role that we want to play.

1

Forgetting About the Past

How Do I Use My School Experience To Guide My Parenting?

What was hard to bear is sweet to remember.
- Portuguese proverb

Our Memories Frame Our Experiences–School has Changed, Our Memories Haven't

Education is unique in that everyone with whom you interact with has a basic understanding of the education process and how schools operate. Everyone can draw a mental image of that one teacher who made a positive, or not so positive, impact on our life. Whether our experience was one that can be described as homecoming queen, high school dropout, or somewhere in the middle, we all have memories of school.

Some of our school memories are consistent, yet many are not. That is, if asked, most of us could describe the classrooms in which we learned with relative ease, and those descriptions would be strikingly similar: wooden topped desks in rows, chalkboards, and textbooks with our name written on the front cover. But that's where the similarities end because, for some parents, the memories bring back amazing moments, remembering teachers who hugged you on the way into the class each day and trips to the library to hear stories about cute monkeys and men with yellow hats. For other parents, the memories are more painful. Memories like being sent to the office for not having a pencil, a teacher who cared so little she let you sleep through class every day, or the teacher who yelled at you for being so stupid.

Either way, positive or negative, your memories of school are the foundation of how you initially view your child's school. Your child's teacher may be the best in the school, but if you had a negative school experience, your ability to trust and engage in the learning process will be diminished. Without intentional efforts to understand how the past affects your present role as a parent, unintended solutions can arise and impact your partnership and ability to best support your child.

Understanding Schools of Today

Although the classrooms of today still mirror those we hold in our memories, many of the expectations for children (and the teachers) are very different and much more complex. Today's students are required to think differently and produce complex work that will allow them to be prepared to compete for modern jobs. The role of teacher is no longer simply to impart knowledge. Today's teachers also assume the roles of trauma nurse, psychologist, and social worker. This means that our memories and today's reality of school may be so different that it can cause complications, especially with the communication needed to ensure our children experience full success.

Schools today need parents as partners. Teachers need parents to understand how their children are progressing and what they can do to help their children grow. The work of educating children has continued to grow into a 24-hour, multifaceted responsibility for both teachers and families. It is necessary for parents to actively engage with and in the school. It is helpful when parents understand subject matter or assist their children in finding solutions to problems. Understanding that learning demands are drastically different today allows parents to also support their children fully.

The work completed by freshmen in high school in the past is being taught to children in sixth and seventh grade today. In the best math classrooms, the expectation for homework is no longer to solve the 50 math problems on a page, but instead to examine the surroundings to learn how the equation is applicable to their world and to apply their knowledge in real-life situations. This shift in learning from practice to application holds true for all subjects in quality classrooms. This requires different teachers, different leaders, and different parents.

As partners, it is essential for parents to move beyond the past so as to best support your child's school experience. This begins by acknowledging that schools, teachers, expectations and even the students of today are different from those in our memories. Consider these deliberate acts to unpack your past. They will help you to be successful in partnering with the schools of today.

Own Your Past. Think about your experiences as a student. Seek to understand how your experiences at school form your opinions of the school your child attends and the teacher with whom they work. Understand that your child is not destined to have the same experiences. Their schooling can be much more positive and the school can do a better job of addressing each and every need they have.

Tell Your School Story. The best way to help others at your child's school understand your perspective is to have an honest and open conversation about how your school experiences made you into the person you are today. If you are hesitant to call the teacher because you view them as the expert and not one to be questioned, tell her just that. Tell the stories that explain your behaviors so you can work to define a partnership that will work for those on both sides of the equation.

Seek to Understand Your Role. Your partnership with the school is a key component to your child's success. Understand that schools want and need you. Find ways to communicate with the teachers and staff at the school that lets them know you care. Regardless of your past, understand that today you are the parent and your child's attitude and perception of school is formed partly by how you talk about school in your home.

Trust. Although there are certainly some bad apples, most folks don't choose education as a career to become wealthy; they choose it because they care about children and our shared future. Trust that the teachers, like you, want the best for your child, even though this may not have been your experience.

Open Your Home. Sometimes experiences are so painful that we simply can't move past them. If you just can't seem to cross the threshold into a school building again, let teachers and staff know they can visit you at home or another place beyond the school.

Even if you had an amazing school experience, this can impact your school partnership as a parent. You may be seeking parallel experiences that no longer exist. Your excitement may apply the wrong pressure to the school and your child. No matter your experience, here are some things that parents have done to grow their school partnership.

Visualize the Past

Allow yourself to visualize the best and worst parts of your time in school. Think about what made the experiences memorable. Look for similarities and differences and allow that to transform your ideology of schools. As your child talks about school, use the wisdom of your years to help them to unpack and troubleshoot the experiences similar to those in your past to get even better results.

Visit the Spaces Again

As an adult, walking the very halls that caused you so much pain in the past, can help redefine your mental image of school. With adult lenses, the hallways aren't nearly as long, the desks quite as large, and the teachers not so untouchable. A renewed view of the physical space can assist with the mental transformation that is so important to your role as a parent.

Understand What School Today Means

Knowing that school for you was most likely a very different experience than what your child is experiencing can help you to understand the new expectations for success. Talk with your child about your memories and how school has changed. Help your child confront problems and create solutions with your wisdom and experiences.

Pay Attention

Check the backpack. Let your child know that school is important to you by reading materials that come home. Listen to the robo-call messages. Talk to your child about the news and events shared. Ask your child questions about their day and what they are learning, not just: "How was your day?" All of these areas will grow your knowledge of today's schools and allow for you to grow as a partner with the school.

Other Considerations

You may think back to your time in school and have a difficult time remembering any "involvement" from your parents other than the occasional parent/teacher conference. Though this may have been tradition and reality in the past, the complexity of schools makes the need for more frequent, quality connection a necessity. Because of this, schools are much more committed today to finding a way to bring everyone into the fold to help every child find success.

Some parents claim that, "I can't support my child in school, I don't have the time or money to do so." For many, this is a real perception on how they view supporting schools. Some parents work full time and can't take time off work to visit the school during the day on a regular basis. Many parents also worry that teachers won't think they are involved if they can't volunteer to go on field trips, cover lunch duty, or send in supplies each month. The reality is that school staff value YOU. You know more about your child than anyone. Knowing what makes your child happy and how he or she is motivated and sharing that with school personnel is golden, and costs little time and no money.

If you are looking for ways to move away from the past, take action. Consider signing up for the automatic text messages so you can remind your child of the upcoming test. Check their grades each week by setting up an automatic e-mail alert. Offer to assist with tasks you can complete at night. Although small, the efforts will be noticed and your child will know you care not only about them, but about how they perform in school.

A Roadmap to the Case Studies Throughout the Book

As you read the case study below, and others throughout the book, it is important to remember their purpose. They aren't designed as the perfect solution for every school or the right way to address every problem. They are windows into the perspectives of parents, leaders, and teachers. They are designed to showcase some of the difficulty of parent partnerships, and we hope that they generate empathy, compassion and open up new conversations.

FORGETTING THE PAST: A CASE STUDY

Leslie finished her shift at the local hospital, checked her watch, and sighed as she hoped the traffic would cooperate so she'd be in time to catch the blue line that would get her home so she could shower and change before she had to leave to go to Kaleb's school. She dreaded this night every year, the school's open house. The annual school visit made her physically ill. She hated having to step foot in the place that had shunned her when she needed someone to support her the most.

As a child, school had always been tough. It seemed no matter how hard she tried, something kept her struggling; a teacher who never seemed to have the time to help or an assignment that she didn't understand. When Leslie ended up pregnant in her sophomore year, she had never felt so rejected. Constant whispers of irresponsibility and a doomed future were a part of her eventual decision to drop out. Now, having to walk the same halls again with Kaleb, Leslie felt a whole new type of pain. She desperately wanted Kaleb to know she thought that school was important, but hated seeing that her son would have to endure some of the same teachers who pushed her away. She wanted to get in and out quickly and to speak to as few people as possible.

Each year Leslie would receive the obligatory beginning of school call from the teacher, but after that call, no one else at school would call, unless Kaleb was in some sort of trouble or behind on lunch money. She'd do her best to try to keep up with what was happening at the school and with Kaleb's needs, but it seemed she was always one step behind as Kaleb told stories of being left at school because she forgot to pay for the field trip or having to sit in another classroom because when he tried to ask a question the teacher thought he was talking to be disruptive. Leslie still hated school.

This year, as Leslie walked the schedule with Kaleb, counting down the minutes until they could swiftly exit, Ms. Ross, one of Kaleb's teachers, approached. She thanked Leslie for coming and praised the work she had seen thus far from Kaleb. Ms. Ross sensed Leslie's apprehension and gently smiled. She asked Leslie if she could call her later next week to further discuss Kaleb's work and how they could work together. Knowing with certainty that the call would never come, She replied: "Sure." Leslie then walked away, putting her head down so that as she walked by, she would not to have to acknowledge the existence of the very teachers who, in her opinion, had ruined her life.

The following week, as Leslie was closing out her workday, her phone rang. Reading the school's name on the caller ID, she became irritated, wondering what Kaleb had done now or what she had forgotten to do for him. Leslie answered the call to hear Ms. Ross. Following a brief exchange, Ms. Ross explained that, as promised, she was calling to tell Leslie about the essay Kaleb had written in class the past week. "He wrote with such vivid descriptions," Ms. Ross said, "I could see him leaping from side to side trying to straddle the wet cement." Leslie smiled, knowing the story Kaleb must have written about for Ms. Ross. "Your son is a delight Ms. Melton. I enjoy reading his work and learning about him through the little tales he shares with me. I'm calling you tonight to ask if you'd allow Kaleb to read his work in the storyteller's competition we will have in two weeks. I'd like him to represent our school and would love for you to join us." Leslie, heart filled with pride, agreed and reluctantly told Ms. Ross she'd see her there, knowing that it meant going back to the place she hated most once again.

The afternoon of the competition, Ms. Ross greeted Leslie at the door and insisted that she sit with her. The two chatted while the students prepared for the competition to begin. As Leslie answered Ms. Ross's questions, she realized her anxiety was slipping away and she was beginning to feel at ease. She smiled, and with great trepidation, asked Ms. Ross if there was any way she could help in her classroom because she was most grateful for her seeing the promise in Kaleb, and she wanted to pay her back. From the conversations Ms. Ross had with Kaleb, she knew that Ms. Melton had very little free time in her life and that making ends meet each month was already a challenge. So, Ms. Ross said, "I would love your help, but I'm not sure that I need for you to come to school. Instead, what do you think about allowing me to come to your home a few times to discuss how we can help Kaleb continue to grow? I know you work long hours so maybe we could chat over a pizza or something."

Over the course of the semester, Leslie and Ms. Ross talked a few times at the family's home over pizza. Leslie found herself weaving questions about how to help make sure Kaleb graduated into their talks. She wondered often where she'd be today if she had known then that some teachers cared and truly wanted kids to succeed. Regardless, time passed and at the open house that next fall, Leslie was able to walk through the doors of the school with her head held a little higher, knowing that there was another, better school experience for her son.

Summary

Forgetting about the past and the experiences that formed our perceptions of school isn't easy. For those whose school experiences were less than satisfactory, the emotional trauma may still exist for them today. Perhaps we should have titled this chapter "Learning to Tolerate School" because, once our perception has formed, it is possible that perception will exist forever. However, as parents, our role is to find a way to move beyond the past and foster a positive relationship with the teachers and staff that work with our children. We need to withhold judgment and seek to understand classrooms of today, even when the experiences we had are held as negative memories. Even parents with good school experiences have to make a shift to perceive school as a parent. Our role is to model respectful behavior and demonstrate a mutual respect for the adults with whom we entrust our children each day. Above all, we must find our place in the system to best support the growth of our children and allow them to internalize the belief that school matters.

2

Overcoming the Barriers of Partnership

What Steps can we Take to Best Partner for our Students?

Perfect partners don't exist. Perfect conditions exist for a limited time in which partnerships express themselves best.
- Wayne Rooney

The Journey to Partnership is Filled With Barriers

Let's partner. There isn't a school or parent that doesn't want this reality, but agreeing to partner is the easiest part of the journey. Partnership is hard work, and it is filled with potential barriers. This chapter looks at these barriers as a way to remain realistic yet positive about the possibility of powerful partnerships. It showcases why parent engagement has struggled as a movement, and how current cultural demands make recovering these partnerships even more difficult.

Schools need parents and families. They need to make sure that the best parts of learning extend beyond the walls of the school. Schools can begin the process of paving a road to success beyond high school, but it takes other supports for this vision to become a reality. It means having conversations about hopes and dreams. It means having norms and limits that allow learning to remain a priority. These partnerships can truly change the opportunities for students, and they should be the pursuit of all educators and families.

Barriers vary because each school has an individual personality, but there are some commonalities that can be a part of this conversation. Exploring these areas can allow for misconceptions to fade and new connections to grow.

Why Do Barriers Exist?

Barriers are the fruit of misunderstandings. They come when parties make assumptions, judgments, and decisions without all of the information. Parent partnership barriers emerge from these same spaces. In some cases, schools feel as though they understand a family when they only hold a superficial understanding of their realities. They may see a family as connected to the school because of how they show up at events, but life at home includes taking care of a dying parent or grandparent. They may see a family that lives in a small home and judge their economic situation to be one where ends barely meet. Families may see a school that doesn't care because of an incident that they heard about a few years ago or based on the appearance of the school from the outside.

Barriers emerge from tradition. Schools get in a rut about how they communicate, and families get in a rut in how they participate. Neither of these approaches are healthy as these ways fail to change to meet the current realities. Barriers also come in physical, digital, and attitudinal forms, and every school has room to improve one or more of these areas to support students. Consider whether some of these barriers exist in your school/home partnership.

Physical. How easy is it for parents to gather at the school both inside and outside of the building? Does the school feel like a welcoming place or more institutional in how it receives individuals? Does the building make families feel both safe and cared for?

Digital. Is it easy to find a teacher's e-mail address? Do communication strategies include a variety of media including texts e-mails, and calls? Is the website useful, filled with quality information? Does the school use appropriate social media to support greater transparency and trust?

Attitudinal. Do you feel like you have a valued voice in the school? How does it feel to be a part of the school community? Is there an energy that is genuinely positive around partnering with parents? Can you feel a warmth from teachers and leaders?

If you answered any of these questions with a no or with less than a resounding yes, consider these first steps in removing some of the barriers between families and teachers and school leaders.

First Steps

- NAME IT: The first part of overcoming a barrier in parent partnerships is to name the barrier. Naming the barrier isn't about blame, but it is acknowledging that there are things that are impeding greater success.
- CAPTURE THE BARRIER IN IMAGES: It is often difficult to articulate the things that are getting in the way. We see them and feel them, but the words can be hard to come by. Try to capture the barrier in pictures, so that a conversation can start around something that is concrete and less abstract.
- LOOK FOR SOLUTIONS: Barriers in schools often have been solved in other schools. They may be new to you, but often someone has tried one or more solutions in the past. Start with these as a frame going forward.
- BABY STEPS: Barriers weren't built in a day, and they won't go away overnight. Barriers are often unintended habits, and chipping away at habits takes time. Work between the school and families to unify, taking baby steps on both sides.
- CELEBRATE SMALL WINS: Bringing down barriers between families and the school is essential for strong partnerships. To make this happen, don't forget to

celebrate the wins. Celebrating builds momentum, and it creates a pause that builds capacity, will, and energy for the next bit of hard work needed on the partnership journey.

Other Considerations

There are a number of other areas that can create barriers between school and home. Some of them are obvious while others require some reflection and introspection to see how they manifest within the school culture. Small barriers can have a big impact on learning. They become the pebble in the shoe that nags and nags until it is easier to go without the partnership at all. Teachers, leaders, and parents can all be on the lookout for these barriers.

The Information Barrier

In a noisy world, when parents are trying to make it through all of their day-to-day decisions, information about school opportunities can get lost. Partnership means creating a communication bridge that works for the family and the school. What is the best mix of communication media for the partnership? Have schools asked parents? Have parents discussed their preferences? Does anyone listen to automated calls? Are texts costing families money? What percentage of e-mails are opened and read? All of these questions should be considered in order to bridge the information barrier. Parent partners want more information. They want a sense of transparency. They want to know what is happening. Schools can do much better in personalizing the way communication occurs.

The Role Barrier

What is my role as a parent? The answer to this question may seem easy, but many parents are seeking a more nuanced role. This role includes being supportive to the work of the school both with their child and in the neighborhood. It means advocating for all children when you see an injustice or decision that impacts students unfairly. This new nuanced role is also one of aiding with homework, attendance, and more. It is also a role of question-asker. How is my child doing? How can I help them grow? How will I know when they are successful? Most parents don't know how to activate all of these roles. Most parents perform the one or two roles where they have been successful. The barrier to deeper partnership is in the expansion of roles.

The Comfort Barrier

As a parent, am I comfortable at school? Do I feel like everyone is truly seeking friendship instead of just trying to be nice? Are there other parents at the school that I have tension with? Do I feel comfortable in the community or does every appearance feel like I'm being judged by hundreds of sets of eyes? All of these are questions that many families tackle as they try to grow as partners with the school. In addition, some families have felt success in school buildings and others haven't. This impacts what it feels like when they come to school to partner. Comfort also comes when a student feels welcomed and loved.

The Access Barrier

Partnership is loosely associated with access. Not all parents are recognized by their face at the school. Some parents are just a name and phone number on a registration form. Finding new ways for access and visibility can include high levels of intentionality around events and activities that allow more and different parents access to the school and partnership.

The Time Barrier

Our busy world inhibits parent partnerships. This is true for parents working three jobs, the parent with a job that requires lots of travel, and parents having life demands that absorb a large amount of time like caring for the health of family members or caring for their own mental health. Partnership can be served in small doses, but schools have to consider this time barrier in new ways, so that they can shape the concept of partnership. Thirty minutes a month in an asynchronous way can add up to a huge value add for the school and the growth of a child.

The Relationship Barrier

When I walk into a school does anyone look like me? Does anyone really know what I'm going through? Does it feel like a place that really loves my child? Building relationships is hard work and can be damaged with the slightest comment, action or inaction. Many parents don't see themselves at school; they don't see others of the same race or economic status. They don't see the people who live in their communities. All of these things create tension, and when there is tension, partnership is less fruitful.

The Complacency Barrier

When parents send their children to a "good" school that has a strong "grade," there is a tendency to believe that they have completed their job in the partnership. The trouble with this is that so much more is possible. Excellent schools are always continuing to grow, and they recognize the need for additional human resources and support. They need parents who ask questions. They need parents who tell their school's story in the community. The barrier that develops here is that parent trust is too high and they tune out the information coming home because they perceive things to be good. Partnership is a daily activity, and this subtle barrier impacts what could be possible.

THE EASY PARENT: A CASE STUDY

Rodney always thought that he would be an easy parent for a school. He made sure that his daughters lived in a good neighborhood. He made sure that they went to school most days, and he stayed out of the school's way. He had confidence in the school and an attitude that the school served its purpose. The school could reach out to him if they needed something, and he would respond, He attended enough events a year (one or two) that the teachers and principals knew to which child he was connected.

Rodney wasn't interested in being a parent who caused trouble or asked a bunch of questions. He realized that he wasn't going to be the primary parent partner in his family as his travel schedule with work limited his day-to-day involvement in school. He cared deeply about his daughters and their learning, but he recognized that school wasn't the only place that they would learn, and, he paid for plenty of activities to support learning outside the school walls. Rodney had less time than some parents to be actively involved. He didn't feel guilty about it, but it also meant that he wasn't looking for ways to connect with the school either.

A few years ago, Rodney had been involved with a high profile bankruptcy of his business in the community that led to a number of people losing money and jobs. Ever since, it has been difficult for him to be in the community. There are still lots of glares and side conversations about him at local restaurants and when he does visit the school. Rodney knew that he needed to be connected to the school for his daughters, but he was still wounded by the fact that he had injured so many in the community. He didn't want anyone in the school to take frustrations that resulted from his actions out on his daughters. Coupled with this lack of comfort, Rodney didn't really know his role at the school. How could he actually be helpful? What role for him existed outside of open house, conferences, and holiday parties? With no clear role, he sunk into passive parenting mode and took on a "do no harm" philosophy.

This philosophy led to a complacency that dictated his reality as a parent partner. He slowly grew more comfortable in this role, and it allowed him to think about other things that impacted his life including fitness and the family finances. Recently Rodney started playing basketball in a men's league in the neighboring community (it was easier than playing in his community because of all the extra complications). The principal of his daughters' school also played in the league, and they had a chance to connect one Thursday night after the game. The principal recognized Rodney, and Rodney was surprised.

They ended up talking for a bit, and the principal asked why Rodney wasn't helping with an upcoming project that the school was doing in the community. Rodney apologized for not knowing much about the project, but he said that he was open to help if he was in town. The principal knew most of Rodney's story, and how it was hard for him to be at the school, so, in an effort to be understanding, was quick to let him know that there wasn't any pressure to be involved. Rodney's schedule eventually allowed him to be a part of a Saturday clean-up crew in the park with the principal. This group of five dads, who had similar stories, started to talk about how difficult it is to be a partner with the school. The principal was quietly listening to every word. The great part was that all of the dads had jobs where they created solutions for a living, so Rodney and the others were quick to move from problems to solutions.

They talked about starting a dads' advisory group where they could talk openly about their hopes and dreams for the school. They didn't want to be critical or cause a mess because they hated when people did that in their world. The principal was shaking his head yes. He wanted new voices and new ideas. He wanted to know what business was truly looking for in graduates. He wanted to make sure that dads felt comfortable in the building and didn't have to always be there when the noise of the school was everywhere. The principal also talked about new and different types of roles.

The dads continued to talk while they cleared the park of limbs and leaves from a recent storm. They talked about how they saw the school as a good place. They saw it as a place that they could confidently send their son or daughter, and they didn't see or know a lot about how it could change. The principal knew from this conversation that he needed to come up with a message that resonated. He needed parents to have a sense of urgency around the growth journey that he envisioned. He tried a couple of ideas with the dads. He may have even found something that resonates. He knew he needed a message for dads, moms, business partners, retirees, and more. The principal knew this type of message was extremely difficult to craft, but essential to parent partnership.

Finally, the dads talked about the need for bite-sized partnership. What could they do in 30 minutes once a week? What could they do from a plane? What could they do once a month? They wanted the principal to know that their busyness wasn't a sign that they didn't want to be a part of making the school a great place, but they needed lots of small ways to contribute. The principal started thinking of a variety of possibilities, but he knew that he would need Rodney and others to be a part of the conversation in an ongoing way to maximize their partnership going forward.

Summary

Barriers can be overcome. There isn't a partnership with any family that isn't possible. It isn't easy and the solutions can be complex, but it is essential for today's leaders to enlist the help of all parents to maximize the learning experience of students. Think beyond the cliché of why parents and families aren't involved and dig into solution making that gets to some of the core barriers described in this chapter. Doing so will bring many amazing parents out of the shadows and into the fold for growing the modern schools that everyone is pursuing.

3

Trusting Your Learning Community

How do I Know that the People in My School are Trustworthy?

To be trusted is a greater compliment than being loved.
- George MacDonald

Trusting the People who are with My Child Each Day is Important

There is nothing quite like that first day of kindergarten; waving goodbye as the bus pulls away or a quick kiss as you turn to leave so she doesn't see the tears welling in your eyes. Hope for a successful day fills your thoughts as you watch the minutes tick by until the day is over and your baby is securely in your care again, only to repeat the process over again the next day. Ultimately, the tears subside and the minutes ebb into a routine for your family.

The uncertainty and anxiety that consumes parents on the first day of kindergarten is legitimate. Each year we leave our child with different people, strangers, granting them our trust merely because of their position. In many cases we have blind confidence in the teacher because the opposite would drive us insane. The system of schooling has conditioned us to believe that schools, and the people inside, are trustworthy and safe. This is almost always true.

School personnel are charged with the responsibility of acting *"in loco parentis,"* a Latin term that means "in place of the parent." Schools are responsible for making decisions and acting in the best interest of children. This could mean anything from warmly greeting students at the door each morning to providing a nurturing environment. It could also mean making decisions about medical care in an emergency situation where the child's welfare, or even their life, would be jeopardized by taking the time to contact the parent. This chapter will help to identify characteristics of teachers and classrooms that we believe should instill a sense of confidence and trust that is based more on relationships than positions.

What Makes Someone Trustworthy?

Trustworthiness is defined as "worthy of confidence; dependable." Certainly there is a hope that the folks who work with our children each day have some basic "trustworthy" characteristics. However, folks in schools have "formal authority." That is, because they are perceived as "in charge" there is an automatic level of respect and trust because of their position. Since we all have the common experience of "school"; we understand the role of the teacher, the principal, etc., and how their position fits in the hierarchy. When asked to complete a task you would do so out of compliance, because someone in authority told you to do so. You *obey* these people but don't necessarily *trust* them. Then, there are others who have "informal authority": these are the folks for whom you have respect because of your relationship with them. Think of your favorite coach or teacher, you would bend over backwards to please that person; you both *obey and trust* them unconditionally.

School people with informal leadership are trustworthy because they have specific behaviors and aspects of character that communicate trustworthiness.

Behaviors. When interacting with trustworthy people, they are consistently kind, compassionate, and humble. Their body language is open, they maintain good eye contact, and it is abundantly clear to you that they are fully present in the conversation. Their interactions with you seem authentic and honest; you can tell that they aren't "faking it."

Ability. We trust people who know what they are doing and are skilled in their trade. Skilled educators understand both children and their curriculum. They are resourceful, they know how to solve problems, and ask questions when needed.

Character. Trustworthy people have good character. They act with integrity and intention, they are consistent, reliable, and committed to not only the task at hand, but to the greater good. Students will describe these teachers as "fair."

Behaviors, ability, and character are showcased in a variety of ways at school. Below are a few of the ways that parents can begin to see them in action.

- SHARED DECISION MAKING: When establishing trust with families is a core value, all stakeholders have a part in making decisions about planning for school improvement, funding, and staffing. Parents are genuinely valued as thought partners rather than as a signature to fulfill a requirement.
- UNDERSTAND CURRICULUM: Trust educators who not only understand the material they are responsible for imparting, but those who are able to help parents understand what is being taught and can provide resources to allow parents to be partners in learning.
- TRANSPARENCY: Trustworthy educators are transparent. There is no "dog and pony show" with these folks; what you see is what you get. They are intentional in their conversations, no matter the topic. Conversations are from the "student lens." Trustworthy folks genuinely have nothing to hide, even when they are at fault.

- REGULAR, MEANINGFUL COMMUNICATION: Families want to be informed about what is occurring in the classroom. In places where trusting relationships are central to the philosophy, open and honest communication is plentiful. Communication is two-way and occurs in a variety of ways, not just a monthly newsletter home or a robo-call on Sunday nights. Options exist to meet all communication needs. The communication is holistic and paints a complete picture of your student and the school.
- NO HOLDS BARRED ATTITUDE: When parents are valued and trusted as partners in learning, schools exhibit a no holds barred attitude toward communication and student achievement. Staff will do whatever is necessary to ensure students succeed and the family is with them every step of the way. This attitude can look like a teacher who asks to visit your home as a way to welcome your child to school or a principal who ensures there are funds to allow every child to go on a field trip, not just those who can afford it.
- MEANINGFUL OPPORTUNITIES FOR INVOLVEMENT: When you are welcomed into the school with open arms, at any time, with no appointment, trust is pervasive. Parent involvement extends beyond traditional planned events like Muffins for Mom and Doughnuts for Dad.

Other Considerations

Sometimes there are cultural differences around respect and trust that can be blind spots for school personnel. By helping staff to understand your needs and expectations as they relate to culture, you can help build their cultural capacity as well as ensure you establish an open, trusting relationship with the school.

Bad reputations are the result of a negative story and experience "going viral." Teachers make mistakes, but parents who are partners recognize that we are all fallible and should have the opportunity to recover and repair damages. Having a positive attitude and assuming best intentions as a parent partner demonstrates a willingness to step into the vulnerable space of trust.

Reputations play a role in establishing trusting relationships. Being cognizant that what you hear "on the street" may only be one person's truth is an excellent way to form a bridge toward a trusting relationship. Also, being diligent about seeking the truth from the source sends a message of concern and care.

Students and their parents also carry reputations. Making efforts to understand how you and your child are perceived can help you shape your relationship with the school and establishment. Healthy partnerships also wipe the slate clean to rebuild the foundation of a trusted partnership.

In conclusion, there are just bad first impressions. Every person carries invisible baggage that sometimes spills out into the present. This may mean that at open house the teacher didn't greet you and your child with a smile because their family pet died the previous day. Or, your child is the one who is known as the kid who sleeps in class and hides food in his locker but you kept it hidden that you were homeless for six months during the previous year. Working to understand the difference between a bad first impression and pervasive issues that could negatively affect teaching and learning provides all parties with the benefit of the doubt to establish trust. Kindness and compassion are cornerstones to trusting relationships between schools and families.

BUILDING TRUST: A CASE STUDY

Isabella watched as the school bus carrying the teachers made its annual trip around their neighborhood. New faces gazed intently out the window as they did each August before the school year began. "Another school year, another year of looking at us like we are fish in a bowl," she thought as her children played outside, waving at some familiar faces from years gone by. Isabella shook her head, smiling because she felt so lucky that her children loved school and had experiences thus far that had been relatively positive. She continued preparing dinner as she listened to the nightly news from the television.

Isabella had called the children, Sofia and Sebastian, in to wash up for dinner when there was a knock at the door. Not expecting visitors and dinner waiting to be served, she reluctantly answered the door. At the door was one of the new faces she had seen peering from the bus window. "Good Evening Ms. Hernandez, I'm Natalie Simmons and I'll be Sofia's teacher this year. Do you have a few minutes to talk to me?" the face said. Completely surprised, Isabella invited Ms. Simmons in and asked her to sit while she put dinner momentarily on hold.

While Isabella was in the kitchen, Sofia and Sebastian came back into the living room. Ms. Simmons introduced herself to the children as Isabella heard a squeal from Sofia, "You're MY teacher?" The excitement of having Ms. Simmons in her home was evident. As Isabella walked back to meet with Ms. Simmons, Sofia ran by, saying something about a glass of water.

The women sat and Ms. Simmons thanked Isabella for taking a few minutes to speak with her. She explained that she was new to Clay Elementary School and wanted to get to know her students to help them ease any nervousness about having the "new teacher." Ms. Simmons shared her teaching experience thus far and bit about her own family with Ms. Hernandez. She then asked a few questions about the Hernandez family and in the process learned that Matthew, Isabella's husband, had been recently deported due to a mix up with his immigration paperwork. Ms. Simmons gleaned that the family was struggling without Matthew both financially and emotionally, although Isabella presented a positive outlook and confidence that he would return before the year's end.

As Ms. Simmons prepared to leave, she handed Isabella a few papers. As the papers exchanged hands, she told Ms. Hernandez that there were three items: a note from her welcoming Sofia to her class, a list of supplies she hoped students would be able to bring to class, and an assignment for Sofia to complete before the first day of school. Ms. Simmons grinned as she heard Sofia groan from the other room. She thanked Isabella for welcoming her into her home and walked a few doors down in the apartment complex to talk with her next family. Isabella quietly closed the door and walked back to the kitchen to finish dinner preparations as she thought optimistically that this may be Sofia's best year yet.

The first day of school eventually came, and Sofia and Sebastian eagerly boarded the bus to Clay Elementary School. Sofia, excited to see Ms. Simmons again, clutched her homework assignment in her hand. The first day came to a close and the children returned home. Each child handed their mother a thick packet of forms to be completed and returned to the school the following day. Having learned to expect this barrage of paper, Isabella grabbed a slice of the pizza that she had brought home for dinner and sat down at the table to begin the chore of answering the same questions she had several times before.

Sebastian's packet was filled with the usual, emergency contact form, free lunch form, PTA membership form, health form, and photo release form. Isabella diligently completed all of the forms and returned the envelope to Sebastian. She then opened Sofia's envelope. This time though, the first page was a note, thanking Isabella for her visit a few weeks ago. Also on the note was Ms. Simmons' business card with her school phone number, e-mail address, and, her personal cell number. Smiling at the difference in the packets already between the two children, Isabella turned to the next page. On that page were two questions: "What do you want me to know about your child that I don't already?" and "What do you and your family need from me to make this year a success for your child?" Isabella set the paper down, unsure of how to answer, because no one had ever asked her those questions. She flipped to the next page. It was a survey, listing some of the key topics to be covered that year and asking parents to rank possible field trips from one to ten so Ms. Simmons could identify the best fit for student interests and to not repeat trips that had previously occurred. Sofia completed that page with her. There were none of the forms that Sebastian had brought home in Sofia's packet. Isabella looked through Sofia's bookbag to ensure she hadn't missed something and eventually went back to the note on the first page of the packet. The last line of the note said: "Thank you in advance for the time you will spend sharing information with me. It will make me a better teacher for your child. I know many of you have more than one child at Clay, so please look for all the required paperwork from the school to come home tomorrow. Completing one pack a night is plenty. After the home visit, Isabella felt this year would be a different experience, but now she knew that Ms. Simmons was someone special; someone she could trust implicitly with her sweet Sofia.

Summary

For 12 to 13 years, we trust that our children enter schools and classrooms that are filled with caring and nurturing people. We must, however, be able to discern between those we trust because of their position and those we trust because of their behaviors and dedication to children. We should remember that building meaningful partnerships with those who work most closely with our children will result in greater mutual trust.

4

Caring About the Right Things

When Everything is Important, What Matters Most?

From the time we are born until we die, we're kept busy with artificial stuff that doesn't matter.
- Tom Ford

Knowing the Difference between Critical and Important

Thirteen straight years of most children's lives are spent in school. During that time, many parents rely on the school to provide quality experiences that will allow their child to be a productive citizen in the years to come.

Since we all have a frame of reference with regard to what school "looks like," it is easy to look with judgment at the goings-on inside. Thoughts like "oh I could do that better" or "if the teacher would only do this instead" circle in the minds of parents, even though there is no training in educational methodology or child development. We believe that because we know our child best, we also know how they will best succeed in school. When parents are partners in the learning process, a transformation from judgment to inquiry occurs. We begin to increase trust and learn that there are some matters best handled by the school folks.

We learn that creating independence is a must-do for our children to be successful. There is, however, a delicate balance between creating independence and micromanaging your child, the teacher and school. There must be a relationship with the school and teacher that is built on a solid foundation of trust. Parent partners learn that questioning every assignment, communication, or decision is not only unrealistic but toxic to a productive relationship with the school. The reality is that the parent who questions every decision or assignment is perceived not only as a nuisance, but also as someone who doesn't trust the school; they carry a reputation that can cause difficulty in forming relationships.

This chapter will help guide parents in understanding the "big rocks," the concepts and ideas that are the cornerstones for caring about the right things.

The Big Rocks

Knowledge acquisition and learning. When we consider the various aspects of a classroom, we hope that the teachers and staff are preparing our children for a better future. We hope that they are teaching "the basics," but are finding ways to enrich the knowledge and learning with other important skills. Our memories may be filled with images of rote fact recall and activities that required memorization. However, in classrooms today where facts and figures are a keystroke away, the learning should be steeped in curriculum that models inquiry and requires students to practice reasoning, problem solving, and decision making.

Emotional and social skills. Our children live in a digital age. Many of their conversations are bits of data transferred from one device to another or images that are gone as quickly as they were created. To contrast this, classrooms should be places that build and create positive relationships and teach our children how to form these relationships in more traditional ways. They should be places where children understand how to be a member of a team, the value of collaboration and the importance of community. In addition, today's classrooms have to teach children about being aware of how media feeds are defining body image, success, and wellness.

Caring about the "big rocks" is important because if we don't insist on classrooms that look and feel different from the ones in which we were taught, our children won't be empowered nor have the skills to be highly valuable workers in a globally competitive environment.

Classrooms that are attentive to the "big rocks" will also have some other distinct characteristics. Although the things listed below will seem to be common sense and the most basic of expectations, they form a powerful set of characteristics for success.

Safe environment. Above all else, you should feel your child is safe at school. The school should have clearly defined processes and protocols around bullying. It should conduct routine drills for critical emergencies such as a fire, tornado, or an instance requiring the school to be locked down. Playground equipment should be in good working order and not damaged. The ground around the equipment needs to have sufficient and appropriate cover to soften the impact in the event of a fall. Both the interior and exterior of the school should be free from clutter that could cause slips, trips, and falls. Care about safety.

Classroom culture of kindness. Your child's classroom should be one where the emotional well-being of students is just as important as their success on a standardized test. Your student should be motivated by the teacher and the instruction. He or she should like school. The physical space should be inviting (current student work is displayed, clean, well designed), and it is should be crystal clear that the teacher cares about the children. Care about kindness.

Expectations are clear. Whether it is for an in-class assignment, a group project, or homework, students should understand what is expected and how they can be successful. If expectations are consistently unclear, it could be a sign of a deeper issue in the classroom. Care about clarity.

Consistency and equity are present. The best classrooms operate smoothly because the teacher is consistent with both academic and behavioral expectations. Students clearly understand what is acceptable and unacceptable. Although all students may not be achieving at the same level, parents should be able to see that everyone is making progress and support is provided equitably. Care about consistency and equity.

Parent-friendly. Classrooms where there are open doors, and those passing by can see what is happening, communicate an environment of trust. Occasional visits to your child's classroom should be welcomed. Be wary of classrooms with closed doors and covered windows. Wonder what is behind the door and why there is a need to hide. Care about feeling welcomed.

Knowledgeable teacher. The rumor mill of the community often defines the best teachers. A good teacher, however, is one who understands the content and can provide excellent resources to you as a parent partner so you can help your child. A quality teacher is creative in their presentations and assignments. They are patient and compassionate. It matters to them that all children succeed. Care about the quality of instruction.

Feedback. The high caliber classroom is ripe with feedback. The feedback to students is honest and timely. Parents are well-informed about grades and upcoming events. The teacher who knows how and when to contact you is valuable. Care about feedback.

Other Considerations

It is important to remember that equitable and fair don't always mean *equal*. Every child has their own story, and some may need more support than others. There are inequities that exist in facilities, course offerings, and the quality of teachers; parent partners work with the school to eradicate inequity not only for their child, but for all children in the school.

All schools should be teaching children to be culturally competent in an increasingly diverse world. Classrooms that build understanding about the cultures from which all students come are ones where emotional intelligence is as important as technical or intellectual proficiency. Schools should be helping your child understand and interact with people of different races and cultures.

Not understanding the material taught during the day and not understanding the expectations of an assignment are two different concepts. Knowing the difference helps you to provide the right kind of support at home. When a student says, "I don't know what to do," probe to determine if they are unclear about the parameters of the assignment (expectations) or if they don't understand the material well enough to make progress on the assignment (material).

Know that grades don't always matter. Care about whether your child understands what he or she is learning. Pay attention to how points are calculated on assignments. There are times when oversights like not putting your name on a paper or turning in an assignment late are the cause of a poor score rather than a lack of understanding the curriculum.

Ask questions. Please don't get the impression that it is not acceptable to question what is happening at school. We encourage you to operate with trust that the school folks care about your child, yet don't be afraid to trust your parental "gut" as well.

Parents who are also educators, have a more complex partnership to navigate. If you fit into this category, find ways to give extra pause before asking questions. Because you are an "insider," your questions may be deeper and more challenging. This may hit more to the core of the teacher's methodologies. Educator parents often know the response they want before they ask the question. Resist this urge. Educator parents must work extra hard to send the message of partner rather than judge.

CARING ABOUT THE RIGHT THINGS: A CASE STUDY

When Abby found out she was going to be a mother, she and her husband Eric decided they would make a few changes to their lifestyle so Abby could quit working as a banking executive and stay home while their children were young. Having both been raised in homes where both parents worked full time jobs, Abby and Eric both felt the value of her being home far outweighed the salary they would sacrifice.

Abby decided early on that if she was going to be a stay-at-home mom, she was going to be "all in." Each year she volunteered to serve on multiple committees at the school, she offered to be room mother, and visited her children's classrooms several times a week to "help" the teacher. She served on the school's leadership team and coordinated the Family Fun Day held at the school each spring. She had enjoyed watching her beautiful girls, Kasey and Lexi, make their way through Greenhill Elementary and couldn't wait for her baby girl Natalie to start kindergarten in a few short weeks.

One August afternoon, Abby had decided to run by the school to see if she could talk with the principal, Mrs. Murray, as she was dying to know whose class Natalie would be in. Abby wanted Natalie to have Mrs. Vitez, as both of her previous girls had been in her class. Abby knew that Mrs. Murray knew who she was and that she dedicated a lot of time to the school so perhaps she would share the information with her even though it wasn't due to be posted until later that week when teachers returned.

Abby cheerfully entered the school and was greeted by the school's secretary, Kathryn. After the ladies had run down the summer for each of their families, Abby asked if she could see Mrs. Murray. Kathryn asked if everything was ok. Abby replied in a whisper, "Oh yes, I'm hoping she will tell me who my Naticakes has next year." Kathryn acknowledged Abby with a nod and went to the back of the office to see if Mrs. Murray was in her office, as she had been out walking the building with the custodian to make sure the school was ready for the teachers to return.

Mrs. Murray was in and agreed to see Abby. "Hello Mrs. Akers, so good to see you. How can I help you today?" Abby replied, "You know my Naticakes starts kindergarten in the fall, and I was hoping I could sneak a peek at who her teacher will be."

"Mrs. Akers, I'm sorry, I can't share that with you now. You should receive a card in the mail in the next couple days and a call from Natalie's teacher by the end of the day Friday," said Mrs. Murray. Disappointed, Abby told Mrs. Murray she understood and reluctantly left her office.

Since she was at the school already, Abby decided to check the PTA's mailbox in the teacher's area. While she was looking through the stack of mail that had accrued over the summer, she heard some voices talking in the hall. She recognized the voices as those of Mrs. Vitez and one of the other kindergarten teachers, Mrs. Jones. As Abby smiled and walked to greet the ladies, she stopped in her tracks when she overheard the teachers talking about their class lists:

> *"…that's great, she's a cutie. Hey, who has Natalie Akers? Thank goodness Mrs. Murray didn't give her to me. I think one more year of Mrs. Akers breathing down my neck every day may have sent me over the edge," said Mrs. Vitez. "I know," said Mrs. Jones, "I'm glad it's not me! She thinks she is the queen of this place and can come and go as she wants. I had Kasey last year, and I had to have a conference with the Akers after almost every test because Mrs. Akers questions everything. I finally got to the point that I covered my window and closed the door so Mrs. Akers wouldn't stop by."*

Abby covered her mouth so the teachers didn't hear her crying and waited for the teachers to return to their classrooms to quietly slip out without being seen.

She gathered herself and decided to finish her errands. Abby was in line at the grocery store when she saw Julie, her best friend, and one of the teachers at Greenhill Elementary. Julie came over to say hello but paused and asked Abby why she had been crying. Abby did her best to dismiss her tears, as she didn't know how to have a conversation with Julie about what had transpired. Doing as best friends do, Julie persisted. Abby retold the conversation she overheard. Abby said, "Jules, why would they say such awful things? I only ask a lot of questions because I want to understand how the teachers get their scores. I want to be sure the girls are being treated and graded fairly. I visit the classrooms to help the teachers but a lot of times they tell me they don't have anything for me to do so I just sit down and watch for a little while." The ladies both exited the market, and Julie agreed to talk more with Abby about this over coffee later that day.

When they sat down over coffee, Abby was much more composed. She asked Julie again why the teachers would say such things about her. Julie took a sip of her coffee and a deep breath and said, "Abbs, you're my best friend in the whole world, but I wouldn't want you as a parent in my class either. You're so high maintenance." Abby was taken aback by Julie's comment and asked why she had never offered to share this perception with her before. As expected, Julie told Abby she didn't know how to tell her because she knew it would hurt her feelings. However, Julie stepped out of her role of Greenhill employee and into her role as best friend. The friends talked for over an hour about how teachers and staff at Greenhill perceived Abby and her worrisome ways. Heartbroken, Abby asked, "How do I fix this? I have six more years at Greenhill with Natalie, and can't imagine them thinking of me like this that whole time." Julie said, "It's simple Abbs. You've got to trust us. I know you want to make sure the girls are ok, but you have to trust that we are being fair to them. Has anyone ever given you a reason to think otherwise?" Abby shook her head no. "And, we LOVE help. But Abby, you need to talk to Natalie's teacher to find out what she needs and when is the best time for you to help. No one is hiding anything from you. It's just that dropping in all the time disturbs the class when you don't have a purpose. It makes it hard for us to do our job."

As the ladies parted, Julie promised to help Abby build a new reputation this year. She gave Abby a few tips on how to start the year right with Natalie's teacher. Abby promised she'd ask fewer questions and trust more. She wanted teachers to know that she cared about what was important.

Summary

We want our children to progress through life with ease. We learn that allowing them to make mistakes helps them to build perseverance and determination. We understand that in our role as parents we don't have, nor can we ever have, control of all that affects them as they grow. Ultimately though, caring about the right things, the things that create positive learning experiences and reinforce successful relationships, are the aspects of being a parent partner that matter most.

5

Holding Your School Accountable

How Can We Demand Excellence in a Kind Way?

A body of men holding themselves accountable to nobody ought not to be trusted by anybody.
- Thomas Paine

Asking for What you Need and Want

The concept of stress is often seen as negative, but stress can be a positive force in systems including schools when applied in the right dose. While many schools feel the pressure to perform based on state and federal mandates, this is rarely the positive pressure that schools need to improve. Instead, positive pressure that comes from local organizations and parents can be vital for schools to grow. It allows them to reflect and work to incorporate new ideas and push back against current traditions. Parents as powerful partners can begin this work by asking questions about things that don't make sense, talking about the things that they value, and sharing new ideas. This chapter will unpack some of these areas for parents looking for new ways to support schools in their complex work for kids.

Schools need parents who are amazing, strong advocates for their children. This is foundational to excellent parent partnerships, but the key for growing a powerful parent partnership is being someone who advocates for not only their kid, but for all the kids in the building. The language that comes with this level of partnership sounds like this would be great for "all" children instead of this would be helpful for "my" child. This shifting mindset can help a school to grow. It also grows the accountability of the entire school as many more adults are thinking about the overall needs of the learning community.

Are you willing to support the changes that you desire? This doesn't mean more committees, but it does mean completing more projects. Committees and meetings are where ideas go to die. This doesn't mean that there hasn't been a good meeting or a great committee, but these are rare in the world of education. Be cautious about joining a committee as this can often absorb all of your time with lots of talk and no action. The most powerful parents look for and ask for meaningful, short-term action items that they can complete for the school. A series of these short, meaningful items can lead to hundreds of amazing changes.

Questions that Allow for Accountability by Design

Healthy schools are places filled with questions. Students are asking each other and their teachers questions. Teachers are asking students questions. Leaders are wondering and supporting with questions. Parents too can ask questions. How many questions have you asked about your school? This may be a key place of reflection for parents who are looking to grow as partners. Questions are a welcome way of exploring issues that don't seem right. Questions allow for clarification of neighborhood whispers, and questions provide the opening for a great dialogue between the educators serving students throughout the day and parents who serve their child in the remaining hours of the evening. Below we explore five different types of questions that parent partners can ask:

- WONDERING QUESTIONS: "I wonder…" is a powerful question stem that allows for those receiving the question to realize the person asking is truly seeking to understand instead of being sarcastic. "I wonder if we" begins an inclusive conversation.

- "HELP ME UNDERSTAND" QUESTIONS: As a parent, it always makes sense to grow your understanding of the educational process. When you ask for school personnel to help you understand, it humbles your position and draws upon their expertise in developing a solution.
- CLARIFICATION QUESTIONS: Schools assume that parents get chunks of information like puzzle pieces that they use to construct their individual understanding of school. Schools are used to these types of questions and when parents ask about the important issues of learning this leads to greater school accountability about the things that matter.
- URGENT QUESTIONS: As parents, we can't cry wolf, but there are moments when we see or notice something about the school that needs to be addressed for the sake of all kids. E-mail, call or ask for a face-to-face conversation around the urgent questions.

Forming the Right Type of Group

Along with questions, there are other ways that parents can join together to truly advocate for and grow their school community. Though this can be done as individual parents, the possibility of change accelerates when a collective of passionate parents band together in support of all kids. Forming the right type of group to support change means considering a few of the essential elements of excellent parent groups.

Diverse

Too often collective groups of parents attempting to hold their school community accountable approach the work without bringing all of the ideas together. Though this diversity consideration should include gender, race, and levels of education, it should also include people who bring a diversity of ideas around what the school should be and how to get it there. That is, surround yourself with folks who don't all think alike.

Parental Experience

There is something powerful about having had a child who has already moved through the school. The second-time parent at a school has a perspective that is worth incorporating into the accountability alliance. It is also true that first-time parents to a school have a unique perspective that isn't influenced by previous mental models. Look for ways to work with the school leadership and teachers through the power of a varied experienced team.

Networking

Schools that are growing need partners and resources. Parents who are powerful partners work together with schools to find ways to access their personal networks to support the school. Some parents underestimate the network resources that they can bring to the table. Sometimes these resources and talents include individuals who can champion the school in the community or others who can connect with hard-to-reach pockets of the community. One great example of this is parents who serve at churches or other civic organizations. They can help to surround the school with the services of these organizations.

Educational Experience

Being an educator doesn't mean that the parent knows all of the school's answers, but it can be helpful to add parents who are also educators to these networked groups that are attempting to hold school communities accountable. Educators who are also parents can help break through the education language barrier and decode school for parents trying to understand and support. Education experience also helps with the timing of accountability and knowing when things will make the most impact.

Fluidity

Powerful support isn't a stagnant thing. Groups that form can grow too firm in their focus. It is important to keep fluidity in the parent accountability coalition. We should ask does it make sense to add members, split the group into two each year, or roll members off the group annually? Groups, like schools, need fresh ideas and perspective in their work to support and hold folks accountable.

Other Considerations

As parents and schools work together as accountability teams, there are a few other questions that they should consider to help the schools grow:

Who are the critical friends? Leaders need safe places to try new ideas. Great leaders are flush with new ideas, but they often have limited audiences with whom they can communicate. Leaders worry that the beginning of an idea will go public as something that is definitely happening. They also worry an idea will get quick push-back and cause tension even though it is still evolving. Great parent partners can be critical friends for new ideas. They are able to provide feedback without leaking things into the general public that aren't ready to be communicated. This is a valuable resource for leaders growing their organizations.

Who walks the building? School facilities grow in their invisibility. As teachers and leaders walk the halls, the details slide into the background, and they often can't see the small things that could make a big difference in supporting the learning environment. Parent partners can play a positive role in the school in doing monthly walks with the principal to identify areas of growth for the facility. This can include volunteering to help with some of the solutions.

Who comments on report cards and conferences? It is inevitable that schools are in need of revising and revamping long-time traditions like report cards and conferences. These can be valuable tools for feedback and communication when done well, but they can also be vehicles of stifling change and keeping other aspects of the school from growing. As parent partners, it can be extremely helpful to make these areas and other similar school traditions a core area of accountability: these older pieces of school, which seem stable and working because they are familiar, are often inhibiting progress. Ask questions into these things as well.

What questions keep us on track? Many parents have a relatively small list of questions that they feel comfortable asking a school. This can often result in parents falling back to questions about test scores. These questions rarely have easy and satisfying answers; instead the answers are multilayered and complex. Parents may like what they hear, but the answers rarely move the needle on progress. Powerful parent partners work to develop a healthy set of accountability questions and then they share those questions, which empowers additional parents. With new questions come great insight and growth. With new questions also comes an opportunity for old, tired, less useful questions to fall from the standard parent portfolio.

HOLDING SCHOOLS ACCOUNTABLE: A CASE STUDY

Michelle sat in the local coffee shop working many mornings when she didn't need to be in the office. She found herself listening to the community members who gathered there each day to discuss all of the "local news." This was the type of place where people "solved the world's problems" while they slowly drank their coffee. Mixed in with the normal conversations about the weather, economy, and politics were microbursts of comments about the current state of affairs in the schools. Some of these comments were based on nostalgia, but some were based on stories that they have been told by friends, grandchildren, and community members.

Michelle knew that it would be easy for her to dismiss a lot of the banter as she was not only the mother of middle school and high school students in the district, but she was the wife of one of the high school assistant principals. She knew that she had the true pulse of the system. This allowed her to dismiss the coffee shop banter as the "commentary of the ignorant"; that is, until she listened with a different lens one day.

On this day, Michelle was eavesdropping on two women from the community discussing how they wished that they lived in a community that had a greater sense of compassion. The two women worried that, even though everyone in their community was always willing to help in a crisis, in daily interactions, they did not see this same care. They wondered loud enough for Michelle to hear about how they could make sure that the kids in town could grow to understand this. The women discussed how they could work with the schools and churches to support building this sense of compassion.

They also talked about how many of the local tradesman didn't have someone to replace them when they were ready to retire. They started thinking out loud about who they would hire when the main carpenter, electrician, and plumber aged out of practice. They knew that there was plenty of work to do in their town and the surrounding towns if someone was ready to slip into these roles. Michelle started thinking about specific students that she knew that may be perfect to step in. She wondered if the school was aware of this rising community concern.

Michelle was also aware that the community had a proud tradition of having many of their young men and women serve in the armed forces. This could be seen with the memorial in the town square. It could be seen when young soldiers returned in uniform during leave, and it could be seen at times when the yellow ribbons were tied around the trees of many residences in town. Michelle wondered if the schools were being intentional enough about telling the stories of past sacrifice so that students knew the history of their community.

Michelle left that day wondering if there was some wisdom in these coffee shop moments that she often dismissed. Sure people gathered to complain, and many seemed mired in tradition and stuck in the past, but she now was seeing how some of these moments help. They can help a community to see a blind spot or uncover a hidden issue missed because of the speed of the daily grind.

Michelle felt like these conversations were also a generational lifeline, and she shouldn't pass up the opportunity to connect these thoughtful women with a group of students at the middle school. She felt like there was learning to be had on both sides, and she was hopeful that the conversation would eventually move beyond the typical one shot community service project to an intergenerational dialogue that would allow progress and tradition to march in sync. She thought that it may even grow the positive energy between the generations in town.

Michelle recognized that there are nuggets of wisdom in every corner of the community, and that she needs to mine the community for the best of these ideas. It would be a way forward to building compassion, finding apprentices, and supporting the military connections to the community. One year later, the school opened its own coffee shop on campus. It was the student-run business that they had been looking for. It brought some amazing community members into the school space to experience the best that the students had to offer. It gave them hope that a compassionate generation could emerge.

The walls of the coffee house were filled with pictures of heroes past and present including first responders, teachers, and members of the military. In addition to the coffee house, the space also brought craftsman into the schools to begin to discuss their trades. They spent time talking about supplies, solutions, and some of their favorite projects. They also talked about their finances, lifestyle, and their choice to stay local.

Michelle knew that all of this had the potential to make the school better. She realized that some of the conversations in the community about the schools were having a real impact on shaping the narrative in a negative way, but she believed that schools can generate a counternarrative by doing things like the coffee shop as well as listening, acting, and thinking about how to enter into these community conversations with a belief that all voices have ideas to support powerful learning for kids.

Summary

Accountability by design moves beyond efforts to change a culture, but it is designed to help create new ideas and programs that can replace the things that are negatively impacting the system. Shifting culture is a heavy lift for a community. It requires all to be in sync for the greater good of those being served. Accountability by design isn't truly about fixing the current challenges, but pushing for new ways of thinking and doing that will take over for the old ways. Schools spend a lot of time trying to fix problems when they need more time on recreating their culture, content, and overall concept as a learning community.

Parent partners can help this effort by seeing things differently, asking about different things, approaching the school community as a place of common ownership, and seeing that change is a journey made up of thousands of tiny efforts. Accountability can be a central, powerful force for parent partners, and it can propel a school from what it is today to what it can be if it is used in caring, compassionate, inclusive ways.

6

Asking the Right Questions

The Art of Knowing the Right People and Being Involved the Right Amount

You can tell whether a man is clever by his answers.
You can tell whether a man is wise by his questions.
- Naguib Mahfouz, Egyptian Novelist

We Don't Know What They Don't Know

When one conjures the image of school, it is based on our childhood experiences and the visions of a time gone by. Today's children are more complex than ever, requiring a growing set of student services. This can create uneasiness for parents as they try to make sense of the schools that serve their children. Schools continue to have enough of the remnants of education past to help parents to feel as though they understand what is happening, but the new systems and practices go well beyond "this new way of teaching math." These systems require new questions and a new type of parent engagement to make sure children are receiving a learning experience that is second to none.

Today, there are more options than ever for parents. School choice is putting more decision making back to parents about where their kids should attend school. A growing number of options from online schools, charter schools, private schools with vouchers, and a variety of public schools have created a new freedom and responsibility for parents as they work to navigate the system and to understand what is best for their children. In order for parents to make these decisions, they need data. Not only the test scores that are the backbone of how schools are defined today, but the data on the culture of school, the leadership of the school, and the vision for where the school is headed.

In order to gather this data, parents need to ask the right questions, know the right people at the school, and get involved in the right ways. Again, there are traditional ways to do these things, but these traditional ways are losing effectiveness as schools evolve into modern learning places. We can no longer base our questions on a quarterly report card that provides a snapshot of the previous eight weeks. Parents need to be asking proactive questions about the growth of their students in areas that prepare them as citizens. Caregivers need to make sure that the building leadership, counselors, and office staff know their students and the members of their family, so that there is a relationship baseline from which to build. Once parents begin to think about formal learning critically by taking time to learn what they don't know as parents, the parenting approach changes.

Be Known for All the Right Reasons

"I don't mean to bug you, but..." Principals hear parents start conversations with this phrase so many times. It is kind and respectful, but doesn't begin the conversation from a place of partnership. As a parent trying to support the system and all of the children served by that school, it is important to approach every conversation through the lens of being a partner in the work.

Many parents know one of the best questions that they can ask anyone in the school is, "how can I help you?" or "is there anything that I can do to support you right now?" Both of these questions infer that you have a wealth of value to the school. Many parents would tell me they felt bad because the only time that they called the principal was with a question or a concern, but approaching multiple people and asking about how to serve or support them breaks this cycle.

There are many parents who are also worried about "being that parent" meaning the parent is a nagging or helicopter parent who doesn't give their child a chance to learn the value of struggling through something hard. When parents are worried about being overbearing, they overcompensate by pulling back to a point that they aren't known at all.

Being known for the right reasons can mean serving with a smile, a thank you, or having positive energy at the end of a long week. These are all things that you can do with every encounter with the professionals who serve your children each day. They take some intention. They take some practice, but they don't take too much time away from your number one role of serving your family and its needs. All of these efforts also make it easier when the time comes to advocate for your child or another. It also makes it easier when the questions are more difficult and the answers are potentially more painful.

The best way to start being known for the right reasons is to start working at being known. It can start with your next e-mail, phone call, or visit to the school. Making some small shifts will result in big results in reshaping your relationship with the school.

Introduce yourself to the building leadership. Meeting the principal isn't the same as going to the principal's office. Let the principal know how excited you are about some aspect of the school.

Ask the new question. Go to someone who serves your child and ask how you can help them.

Meet those who run the school. This phrase is an ongoing joke that the secretaries and custodians actually run the school. The truth is that they are the operations hub for the school, and knowing them will help you know the school.

Look for a new way to support the school. Remember that this could be a smile, a thank you or bringing your talent to the school. Schools are doing a better job of finding ways for people to serve beyond school hours.

Many dads feel left behind when it comes to school partnership. They may be present at events, but they never feel like they are in partnership with the school. This holds true for other parenting situations as well. Making an effort to try some of the ideas above, along with a few of the ideas below, can continue to be a way of moving to a new and different partnership.

Meet More Professionals Working at the School

Many parents know just their child's teachers, and this limits their ability to connect to the school as well as to be known for the right reasons. Make sure that the principal, assistant principal, secretaries, and some of the other teachers (librarian, music teacher, art teacher) know who you are.

Begin to Smile More and Thank People for Serving Kids Well

A great way to serve your school is with positive energy. Those who work at schools pour a great deal of physical and emotional energy in their work each day, and the small refill from a thank you or a smile can go a long way to maintain a positive school culture.

Ask the Question, "How Can I Help You Today?"

This is the partnership question that assumes parents have a giving role at the school and that you truly want to support the work happening throughout the school for your child and others.

Search for Unique Ways to Serve that Fit Your Time to Give

Not everyone wants to be in a parent-teacher organization, serve at classroom parties, or hang out with other people's kids, but everyone has ways that they can support the school. This could include sharing pictures that showcase excellent learning to others in the community. The community rarely gets to see what is happening at school, and this level of sharing helps community confidence.

Ask the Tough Questions with a Relationship in Place

Schools can lose perspective about their work, and they need parents who can ask WHY things are happening at the school. Asking why from a place of wonder helps the school to better articulate their message and focus on the things that matter.

Other Considerations

Shifting into being a parent who supports and uses the system for the betterment of all kids can be a big change. There are many parents who are known for the wrong reasons, and there are parents who aren't known at all. Neither of these groups have found the sweet spot when it comes to the partnership that truly propels schools forward. Making these shifts will help the school, but many will push back about some of the items described above. Consider the following concerns.

No One Will Pay Attention to Me if I Approach the School with These Strategies

While it is true that educators are busy and bombarded with decisions to be made each day, most of them are searching for new ideas, and they are more apt to listen to their parents than the flood of phone calls and e-mails from vendors. Many parents bring great experiences from beyond education that with a few little shifts could be used in schools and districts across the country. The worst case is that someone hears your idea and stores it away for another time.

Parents have so much wisdom about their children. They have seen them in their most successful moments as well as in their vulnerable moments. They know many of the strategies that lift their spirits, get them out of a funk, or motivate them toward excellence. Classrooms without these strategies are failing their mission to personalize learning for all. Parents may need to be persistent with sharing, but it will make the learning relationship stronger for more consistent school success.

It Should Be the School's Role to Reach Out to Me

Schools definitely have a responsibility to bridge the gap between home and school. It should be a top priority for all school leaders to share in a consistent, thoughtful way through a medium that meets the needs of parents. There are times when they believe they are doing so. They feel that the weekly e-mail covers parent connection with no attention to detail around open rates or responses from parents. Certainly, as a parent, you can wait for the school to get it just right for you, or you can provide feedback about your communication needs. Let the school know if you would rather have a text than an e-mail or if there are times of the day that make the most sense for your communication needs.

Though it is the school's role to initiate quality communication, parents can model the quantity and quality of information that they want from the school. Many parents believe that they are bugging the teacher or principal if they e-mail or call, but what they are truly doing is fine tuning their communication experience with the school. It provides some clarity about your individual needs as a parent. This leads to clear, thoughtful communication between parents and the school.

If the School Doesn't Like Me, they may Take it Out on My Child

This is a statement that has been heard by many teachers and school leaders, and it does probably have some basis in reality, but it isn't the collective nature of educators to have this enter into their decision making. Part of being an education professional means stepping into each moment with a fresh mind and an open heart. No human, not even the superheroes teachers have this perfected, but the rare mistakes shouldn't muddy the communication link between home and school.

Asking the right questions doesn't mean accusing. Asking the right questions doesn't mean knowing the answer before you ask the question. Asking the right questions means that you are open to hearing the answer. Teachers want to be helpful, so starting each interaction with the phrase, "I need your help" goes a long way to shaping even difficult conversations in a way where kids are elevated and honored without getting pulled into tough adult conversations.

ASKING THE RIGHT QUESTION: A CASE STUDY

Lisa was a young, single mother with three children. Each morning she would walk Chris into school and wish him well as the day was to begin. Unfortunately, Chris was performing far below his classmates and struggled with work. As the teacher greeted the family each day, she could see a deep level of concern and uncertainty in Lisa's eyes. During a routine parent/teacher conference that was filled with educational acronyms, scores, and a laundry list of areas where Chris needed improvement, the teacher wrapped up the conference with "and do you have any questions?" Lisa knew she wanted Chris to succeed but didn't know what to ask so she replied "No, thank you, we will try to spend more time helping him at home."

Later that week, the principal overheard Lisa talking with another parent about how she wished she knew what to do to help Chris in school. She was teary as she talked about how he hated school, left most days not understanding what had been covered that day in class, and how he felt like he was one of the "dumb kids." In an effort to assist Lisa, the principal approached and asked her to come to the office. Lisa immediately wiped her eyes and reluctantly followed the principal.

With the two smaller children sitting at the table in the principal's office coloring, the principal asked Lisa to talk about Chris. Lisa shared Chris's disinterest of school, her worry that he was struggling so much, and most importantly, her concern that he would fall further and further behind and eventually be "held back." The principal asked if she had talked to the teacher about Chris. Lisa shared that they just had a conference with the teacher, but didn't understand most of what the teacher was talking about. The principal asked Lisa to give her one question she had about what was happening with Chris. Lisa thought about it and asked, "Why can't Chris read?" The principal replied, "There could be many reasons Chris is struggling with reading. Let's plan to meet with his teacher tomorrow afternoon, and we will talk specifically about his progress. Your job tonight is to write down all the questions you can think of about his reading and bring those with you tomorrow."

Lisa left the office and went home to think about his reading. She jotted down a few questions and shoved the paper in her purse. She was reluctant to attend the meeting tomorrow for fear that the staff would think she wasn't a good mother because she had to ask questions and didn't just know the answers. She worried that the teacher was going to outcast Chris because she had "gone to the principal" when in fact the principal came to her.

The next afternoon came and the teacher, principal, and Lisa gathered to talk about Chris. The principal thanked everyone for attending and asked Lisa if she had her questions. Lisa pulled her questions out and a report that the teacher had given her in the days before and said: "This. I don't know what this means," pointing to the graphs and numbers on the page. The teacher smiled and replied, "Sure, let's go through this, but if there is something I'm saying and it doesn't make sense or isn't clear, I need you to stop me and tell me." Lisa smiled and they went through the report, back and forth, helping Lisa to understand measures of reading like fluency, phonemic awareness, and comprehension.

The next morning as Lisa dropped Chris off at the classroom door, instead of turning to walk away after kissing him she made eye contact with the teacher and said "good morning." The greeting was returned and the two began to chat a little more each day. Lisa began to ask if there was anything she could do to help the teacher. Knowing Lisa had the other children she cared for during the day, the teacher offered small projects like cutting out materials, making packets, and other tasks that could be done as her schedule allowed.

The year ended with Chris still behind in his reading, but now, Lisa not only knew why he was struggling, but had learned to ask questions that helped her understand how to help him grow.

Summary

We have to start somewhere, and starting with questions seems like a great place to reset the parent support model for learning. It means both sides looking at each other and saying that what they have been doing isn't working as well as it can. It means both schools and parents giving a bit and being uncomfortable with trying new things. It means believing that what is best for kids may be more difficult for adults. There are systems and places that are broken and don't serve kids well, but most schools in most places are dedicated to serving families, and they are ready for parents and families just like you. They want your questions. They want you in the schools, and they want to know your name. Being a parent partner is a journey into a new type of learning in schools that reimagines the experience for the kids that walk through the doors each day.

7

Surrounding Kids with the Help They Need

How Do I Know What Resources are Available to Support My Child?

No one is useless in this world who lightens the burdens of another.
- Charles Dickens

Learning about Connections

When we think about parent and school partnerships, there are several models, systems, and frameworks that describe what this could look like when successful. Many are graphically represented with intertwined circles or intersecting arrows representing the relationship between the school, the family, and the community. When we truly talk about hope for our kids in terms of meeting the needs of the whole child, we believe there is so much more that is needed to truly offer both wrap-around services and to fill the experience gap that is present for so many of our children. If we truly considered the social, emotional, physical, and academic needs of children, staffing in our schools would be completely different. Partnerships would be pervasive and services to support our children would be readily available to all.

The needs of children are more than just academic. A core part of effective partnerships is understanding the needs of the whole child and knowing how and where to access resources to meet those needs. Schools would be the nucleus of the community and service providers would be readily accessible. Eliminating the need to have insurance, referrals, and co-payments would send a message that we value not only the children we serve, but what they offer to our future.

So often in our schools, there are two folks to whom parents go for support; the teacher and the principal. In this chapter, other points of contact will be explained to support better access to the connections between the school and community. We want parents to know schools are filled with folks who care deeply about children and are committed to their success, and the specialized focus each can play.

Coordination of Support

Today, the primary function of the school is to meet the educational needs of children and the community supports core and extended needs outside of their education. Within these spaces there are microsystems that work in tandem to support children. Unpacking the connections between educational needs and core needs will help grow the partnership between parents, schools, and the community, as folks can more readily access services to meet the needs of students.

Educational Services and Supports

When schools meet the basic educational needs of children, learning happens. Students experience success on a regular basis. When performance is measured by standardized tests, students perform at levels that label them as "proficient" or better. For these needs to be met, students must receive "services" that allow them to readily access and be successful with the curriculum. As schools work to meet basic educational needs of students, there are various roles people hold within the school. Each of these roles offers a "service" to students and families and can help bridge gaps in learning that sometimes prohibit students from maximizing their access to curriculum and learning while others focus on the social and emotional well-being of students. In the section below, various roles are described.

Classroom teachers. Classroom teachers are almost always the "go-to" for parents. They are the ones with whom their children work most closely. The primary role of the teacher is to understand the curriculum and present it in a manner that is engaging and encourages active learning. Teachers are specialists in pedagogy, the art of teaching to learn. So many times though, teachers are called upon to provide other services to support students. Those activities, although important, compound the already complex task of planning and presenting material so that students of all abilities are able to experience success.

Learning specialists. Most schools contain other instructional and support staff who can help parents meet student needs when they are struggling with accessing the curriculum. Schools have teachers specializing in working with learning disabilities, supporting those who are advanced learners, helping students who speak a language other than English as their first language, and teachers working exclusively with students struggling with reading or math. When parents pose questions or students exhibit the need for additional support, it is these learning experts to whom the classroom teacher turns for guidance, support, and advice. These folks are often not in the forefront of one's mental image of school personnel, but they play a valuable role for supporting learning. As partners, parents should feel free to access these staff members for guidance and expertise as readily as they do the child's classroom teacher.

Psychologists. Not to be confused with school counselors, psychologists are often in schools as itinerant or contracted staff. School psychologists are licensed professionals who work with school personnel to assist in the diagnosis of learning differences such as autism, emotional and behavioral disabilities as well as other specific learning disabilities. Most schools have a fully prescribed process by which a student would work with a psychologist, and it is usually following a lengthy intervention process. Parents who are partners understand and welcome the expertise a school psychologist can bring in their deep analysis of a child's learning. They are comfortable seeking answers to the hard questions because, in the end, the child will benefit.

Principal. The role of the principal is often summarized as the "boss" of the school. Although managing the overall operations of the school is certainly one of the roles of the principal, their primary role is to be the lead (or principal) learner. Most principals today left the classroom because they felt a deep and urgent call to affect change in a way greater than they could within the walls of their single classroom. Principals are dedicated to student success and must spend time in classrooms observing, coaching, and providing feedback to teachers to continually provide an environment where everyone is growing. Frequently, principals are thought of as the point of contact when something goes awry. Great principals will encourage parents to talk with the teacher, bus driver, cafeteria worker, etc. to try to solve issue first rather than stepping in and ruling on the matter. Great principals certainly must be accessible to parents, but in a parent partnership, principals are a member of a larger team where all members bring strengths to the table.

Counselors. The school counselor is one of the hidden gems in schools, having a wealth of knowledge about so many things that can positively impact students. This member of the team is focused on personal, academic, and career development so that students are prepared to be productive and contributing members of society. The counselor is a source of interventions when students face challenges socially and emotionally. This could look like anything from having trouble getting along with friends, frequent misbehavior in the classroom, or coping with a family that is unraveling. The counselor also offers career guidance to help children begin to identify how their personal interests and strengths translate to real-world jobs. Family partnerships engage with the counselor as often as possible since their work ensures children emerge as well-rounded, emotionally stable adults.

Social workers. Another hidden gem in schools is the social worker. The work of the counselor and social worker is typically very intertwined. Both are concerned with the social and emotional aspects of the children. The social worker, though, is primarily concerned with helping families to get services when there is something interfering with learning, often acting as the "bridge" to accessing community and other resources. Partnerships, where parents realize the strategic work and the value of this position (and know how to access him or her) decrease the time students and families are in crisis and can more quickly return to a state where they can learn more easily.

School resource officers. SROs occupy a unique space in the school community. Frequently, these folks are employed by the local law enforcement agency, but serve in our schools. School resource officers exist to protect the students inside the school from issues that would negatively impact their health and safety. These issues could potentially interfere with their ability to learn if left unattended. SROs are valuable to schools and the community because, when operating at their best, they have a pulse on the who and what as it relates to school threats. SROs should be accessible to families to assist with any of these issues and much more.

Holistic Family Support

Supports from the community address issues that relate to meeting basic family needs. These organizations and the people who work for them understand the importance of education but also focus on making sure families have their basic needs of food, shelter, and clothing met. Students who lack these vital components of health and safety have, understandably, a difficult time focusing and learning. A brief description of some of the services available is provided below. Knowing which agencies are available for support can break down another barrier that negatively affects our children.

Health services. It is imperative that children receive proactive health care. This includes all aspects of their health, from regular physicals, and annual dental and vision screenings to mental health care as needed. Ensuring that these visits are scheduled is challenging even for the most organized parent. When lack of time and stretched finances make meeting these basic needs even more of a challenge, families can access care through local agencies. Many private service providers offer reduced or pro-bono rates for families that qualify. Having a commitment to seeking quality care is one action parents can do to ensure their child is physically ready to learn.

Social services. Unfortunately there are times when families are not able to make ends meet, and they need assistance. Although named differently in each community, most have a department that can access temporary financial support for vital resources such as rent, electricity, and food. SNAP (Supplemental Nutrition Assistance Program) and TANF (Temporary Assistance for Needy Families) are available when families meet eligibility criteria. These resources can sometimes make an immeasurable difference for families.

Churches and food pantries. When children are hungry they can't learn. More than 13 million children live in homes where they regularly do not have enough food.[1] In 2016, 44 percent of food stamp recipients were children.[2] More and more local churches and community agencies are setting up food pantries where families can access food to ensure they are able to eat. In larger communities families can access multiple pantries throughout the month to ensure the battle with food insecurity is non-existent.

Community colleges. Many community colleges offer programs for parents. Programs range from skill specific training to GED (General Equivalency Diploma) programs. Parents who model high expectations for learning set the bar. Modeling commitment to learning and dedication to goals helps children see the value in investing in self.

Civic organizations. Many civic organizations have a deep desire to not only volunteer but to make a difference in their community. Often schools and parents can find folks who are willing to serve as mentors in these places. Making certain children have a positive role model and someone in whom they can confide helps families when one parent is not a regular part of a child's life.

SURROUNDING KIDS WITH HELP: A CASE STUDY

Michael had wanted to be a teacher all of his life. When he was younger, he'd talked about teaching science in high school then coaching after school, but after an experience with the Special Olympics, Michael knew he was destined to teach in an elementary school. During his senior year in college, he was offered an early contract in his local district because there are few men who choose to enter the profession, especially in elementary schools. Michael was ready to make his home at Point Elementary School.

Michael's first year was off to a great start. He had wonderful colleagues who helped him plan dynamic lessons, his principal was supportive and stopped by to observe him often, and he loved his class. Michael started each day with a classroom meeting, a time when his children could share anything that was on their minds, to help them gain focus throughout the day. Over the past several weeks Michael had noticed that one of his students, Evan, was becoming increasingly withdrawn and quiet, not just during classroom meeting time, but all day long.

Evan was bright. When the year started, one of the most endearing qualities of Evan was that he started his day by telling Michael some interesting factoid. Michael loved it. "Hey Mr. B, did you know…" was Evan's trademark opening. But lately those anecdotes hadn't been coming and Evan had been falling asleep in class, even when he was trying his hardest to be attentive, and his grades were beginning to slip. Michael had begun to notice that Evan's clothing was beginning to wear and appear dirty.

Following lunch one day, the cafeteria manager approached Michael and asked if everything was ok with Evan. Michael shared his growing concern for Evan with her and asked why she was asking. "Because for the last three days, I have watched Evan slip the leftover apples and carrot packs on the table into his pockets. He doesn't know I see him, but when I'm out in the hallway he will slip in here and grab a couple of things and rush out. I'm worried," she said.

That afternoon, Michael called Evan's father, Toby, and shared what the cafeteria manager had told him. "I'm very sorry Mr. Barnes, I'll have a conversation with Evan this afternoon. Stealing is not acceptable in our home," Toby said. Michael explained that Evan wasn't stealing, that he was taking food from an area in the school cafeteria where students put uneaten food, but he was concerned because in addition to being hungry, he had noticed many other changes in Evan recently.

Michael heard a deep sigh on the other end of the line. After a long silence, Toby said, "I'm sorry Mr. Barnes. I lost my job right about the time school started. I haven't been able to find one since. Evan knows something is going on, but not that I'm out of work. I've gone through almost all of my savings and my car needs a new water pump so I can't get to interviews. I'm trying to figure out how I can keep us going but can't." Michael, inexperienced in these sorts of situations, didn't know how to help. He said, "Mr. Athan, I'm sorry. I'm not sure what to tell you right now but I will call you back after I talk to some folks here at school."

Michael set down the phone and stared at the wall. He had no idea what to do next. He walked to the office to see Ms. Jarman, the school counselor. He shared Evan and Toby's stories with her and asked what he could do. Ms. Jarman thanked Michael for letting her know this was going on and asked him to keep his focus on Evan and to keep her posted. She told Michael she would touch base with Toby Athan.

The next morning Ms. Jarman called Evan to her office. She was concerned about his mental well-being. The two talked for a while about school and home and how much he missed his Mom. Overall Evan was a very happy child with a heavy heart. She sent him back to class and told him she'd check on him again later in the week.

Ms. Jarman then called Mr. Athan. She told him that Mr. Barnes had shared a little about what was going on with her. The two talked for over an hour and ended the conversation with Ms. Jarman promising to be back in touch in the next couple of days. Ms. Jarman consulted with the school's social worker, who told her they should go to the Athan's home to talk to Toby in person.

Later that afternoon the two ladies were welcomed into the Athan's home. Toby talked extensively about the family's current struggles and goals. Before the time together was over, Ms. Jarman told Toby that she would begin sending home a food backpack with Evan each week. Toby protested until they figured out a way to discreetly get the food home. The ladies also left a list of local food pantries with Toby. They explained the process for receiving support and told him about places he could access food by using the city bus. The social worker slipped out as Ms. Jarman and Mr. Athan were talking and brought back in a bag of clothes for Evan, a bag of toiletries for the home, and a gift card. She explained that the school community believed deeply in caring for families in need. Toby graciously accepted the donations and the ladies began to lay out a plan for Toby to access temporary services until he was financially stable again.

Notes

1 www.nokidhungry.org/who-we-are/hunger-facts
2 http://money.cnn.com/2018/02/13/news/economy/food-stamps-what-to-know/index.html

Summary

Caring for the whole child and family is the work, not only of the school, but of the community. When resources and funds are coordinated and aligned to strategically support families, students are able to maximize their learning potential and an effective family school partnership is no longer a concept, but a reality.

8

Apples to Apples to Oranges–Comparison Done Right

Does Comparing Ourselves With Others Help Our Parent Partnership?

The reason we struggle with insecurity is because we compare our behind-the-scenes with everyone else's highlight reel.
- Steve Furtick

Making the Right Comparisons

It is quite human to compare ourselves to those around us. It is easy to enter a school, look around, and begin to judge your parenting as it relates to the parents who surround you. Many parents also paint a mental picture of the ideal parent, and then make the assumption that most of the parents who fill the halls of a school fit this image. The pressure to make these comparisons is compelling, real, and hard to push back, but it is so destructive to enter into this losing game of parent comparisons. As effective parent partners, it is essential to resist the deflating energy of comparison, but instead see that your unique insight, based on knowledge and life experience, is an essential asset for the school.

Looking for Greener and Greener Grass

Parents are rightfully always looking for better opportunities for their children. This happens in the smallest decisions about what to buy at the grocery store and how we shape the friends that surround our children. This also happens when it comes to school and learning. Parents are looking for their child to grow so that they can live a full, healthy, happy life. Some parents have choice about which school that their child attends, but most attend their local public school. This can leave parents wondering if their school is meeting the needs of their child as they look around and hear from others about different school experiences. Now more than ever, constant social media feeds, showcase images of other kids and their life in full technicolor. It is easy to get caught in the comparison game. While comparison can bring perspective, it can also lead to misperceptions, anxiety, and a sense that your child isn't getting what they need from their formal learning environment. Consider the areas below that may lead to the wrong types of comparison.

- TEST SCORES: The test scores that are released to the public can be confusing and misleading. As a parent, it is good to review your school's performance, but recognize that you are seeing only a few of the important numbers, and without more information, it is almost impossible to make a true apples-to-apples comparison. Comparing two schools with just these metrics can be troublesome.
- TEACHER EXPERIENCE AND DEGREES: Many folks want to talk about the years of experience of their child's teacher or even possibly that they have a masters or another advanced degree. While these things may be helpful in the classroom, they aren't indicators of success for learning. Amazing new teachers are meeting the needs of all kids in their classrooms every day.
- OTHER SCHOOLS: Schools and parents put their best foot forward about their learning community. This includes pictures of the best moments. Every school has its challenges, but the way that comparison with other

schools works is that their best moments get compared to the worst or normal moments at your child's school. If you are really wanting to compare, you have to dig below the surface of what is put on display to find normal.

- PUBLIC OPINION: The perceptions of the wider community about a school are a lagging indicator about the realities of what is happening in those schools. This doesn't mean that public opinion wasn't accurate. It just means that schools are changing quickly. Every year has different kids, different teachers, and different learning opportunities. It can be destructive as a parent to let too much of this seep into your comparisons.
- PERSONAL COMPARISONS: Along with school-to-school comparison, parents can get caught in the trap of comparing their child to others at their school. This goes beyond class and affluence to include things like academic and athletic performance. Resisting these comparisons allows for your child's strengths to emerge and become cornerstones of celebration and success.

While these areas of traditional comparison are ripe for misinterpretation and often produce unneeded parental stress, there are some areas that allow parents to use the power of comparison in a powerful way that will benefit their child.

Comparing the Things that Matter

The most difficult things to measure in schools are often the most important, and it is a school's responsibility to highlight and showcase these areas. This allows all parents and community members to have healthy, rich dialogues about the similarities and differences around schools. These dialogues eventually help kids to learn in robust ways that will prepare them for life after high school and beyond.

Individualization versus Standardization:

When comparing schools consider how much of the learning can be individualized or personalized based on your student's strengths. Can they showcase their learning through a variety of products or only through standardized tests. Can students choose an individual course of study or do they have to take a series of classes that mirror most others.

Test-oriented versus Project-oriented

Life and work is often a series of projects completed with fidelity. Rarely are we tested as adults in the formats that we experienced in schools. Look to compare how often your school allows for projects to drive the learning as opposed to the learning always leading up to a final test. Projects allows for greater depth of learning and grows creativity and the skills to collaborate.

Rows and Desks versus Flexibility

Schools are now thinking more and more about how the learning environment impacts the learning. They are allowing students to design the optimal learning spaces that often include more choice and movement for students. Rows and desks limit the instructional model and resist the opportunity for flexible and agile classrooms. Compare how your school is doing to modernize their learning spaces.

Learning at School versus Learning Beyond School

Not all of the experts needed to help your child grow can be found at school. The best schools are bringing in experts and guest to support the learning journey. They are practicing the idea of having thin classroom walls that allow students to continue with people and ideas in the community as well as bringing the community into the school. Compare how many different "instructors" that your child has for each class. One teacher as the expert isn't a modern learning experience.

Opportunities to Consume Information versus Create New Meaning

Creating, making, and designing are key ways to make learning sticky. It is the goal of incredible schools to make sure that information and concepts learned today aren't lost following the test. Too many schools are using technology tools to help students consume information when excellence truly emerges when students have opportunities to create and showcase their thinking and learning.

Other Considerations

Comparison, cooperation, competition…all of these words and the actions that come with them can have a graceful execution or can be cutting in their impact. As parents that are looking to support and partner with schools in the most effective ways, consider the following questions:

What keeps you from saying the name of your child's school with pride? Every school is looking to build a positive culture and pride in the learning that is happening. Sometimes this is a work in progress, but there are always positive pieces that are emerging. Focus on areas like joy and happiness. Having your child come home from school with happiness and joy can't be discounted. Talk about individual teachers who you see working hard and bringing excitement to learning. Mention to folks how the principal is available and present for students. All of these areas are great first steps to building pride and fresh perceptions about your child's school with others.

What stories do I need to push back against other people's judgment? The power of story can be incredible when it comes to shifting the minds of friends, other parents, and community members. By telling a story that lasts long enough for people to pause their preconceived notions, it becomes memorable and gives them an image that they can call upon to describe the school. Tell stories about students meeting experts, learning outside of school, and trying new things. Emotion cements stories, and emotion shifts judgment.

What facts do I need to push back against other people's judgment? There are made up, old, and inaccurate data surrounding most schools. They come from tales that spread organically, and, unfortunately, they stick. Don't defend the old data. Often repeating old data in an effort to explain cements the misleading information. Instead bring fresh information to the table. Talk about increases and not raw numbers. Enrollment has increased. Attendance has increased. Teacher satisfaction is increasing. This information pushes folks forward and through their previous judgment.

How do I compare my children to others in a productive way? Parents are looking to validate that they have their children in the right school. Using state grades, websites that grade the schools based on test scores, and looking at annual reports isn't always productive. It is certainly the easiest. Consider reading some of the latest news stories about the school district in both local media sources and the district website, tour a building and compare how it feels in comparison to your school, and look at school and district images as these images can help to paint another comparison.

APPLES TO APPLES TO ORANGES: A CASE STUDY

The week before winter break seems like it is always filled with a lot of activities. Ronny enjoyed most of them, including getting together with her high school classmates. Some lived in town, but many returned home to visit family and friends. The evening usually involved a lot of old stories, some talk of kids, trips, and the always busy calendar. The only part of the evening that Ronny didn't like was when they wandered into talking about the schools where their kids attended. Unlike the other conversations, these moments always drifted into everyone bragging about how great their child's learning experience was going.

Ronny knew that everything her friends were saying couldn't be true. Every mom made their school seem like a super school that provided everything for every student in every moment. Ronny wasn't embarrassed about her daughter's school. The school had really great teachers, and her daughter enjoyed learning. She thought the students had a great librarian, and she really thought a lot of the principal. The school was clean. Students were happy, and learning was happening every day that she visited the school.

It was true that the school, serving families new to the country, had a very diverse population, and that it didn't have every extra program that her friends were describing, but she felt like it was a really good place for learning about both academics and how to live in a more diverse world. Her friends talked about every student having a new computer, the orchestra program, how many languages were offered, the trips that kids took during and after school hours, and most importantly, they bragged about the test scores that appeared in the newspaper each year. They were able to point out how their schools compared, and in this area, Ronny knew that her school didn't score as well.

Every year, she returned from these conversations a bit deflated. She wondered if she needed to move to a new community, so that she could have a "better" school for her daughter. The community was diverse in so many ways. It had a variety of housing, local businesses, and ethnic groups. It was a proud community searching for a new identity with big houses, single family homes, and apartments. It was a place that Ronny felt was perfect for showing her daughter the real world in a safe and productive way. Ultimately though, Ronny wanted what was best for her daughter, and this conversation left her doubting.

She knew that her friends didn't have bad intentions, but she also felt like the comparisons weren't fair. Ronny knew that it took some of the immigrant students a bit more time to assimilate and show what they truly knew on these types of tests. She knew that it was hard to measure the benefits of learning in a diverse environment. She knew that some of these other top performing schools didn't have programming for struggling students and students with disabilities in the way that her school did, but it was hard to bring these factors to the conversation with her friends as a way to push back, as some of them didn't see those aspects of her school as adding value to the overall school experience.

Upon the return from winter break, she connected with a mom in her daughter's class, and they talked about how it is difficult to describe the school in which their kids attend. The easy metrics like test scores and available programs don't tell the whole story. They both felt like they needed a better way to compare their school with the others around them. They wanted to be able to brag about their school, talk about the amazing things happening with pride, and not have to endure another winter break gathering that resulted in self-doubt about their schools.

They decided to talk with the assistant principal at the school. He always had so many stories and excitement about things happening at the school. They wanted to know what they should be sharing with friends, family, and the community. His response was both honest and hopeful. He said that they were working very hard to improve the scores that get reported to the state each year, but they have been able to showcase amazing growth in all students over the past two years. He wished that they showcased this type of growth in the newspapers. He noted that the shift to a more active, student-centered learning environment has reduced absences, increased students' excitement about school, and it has allowed more students to participate in virtual field trips and collaboration among classes. He said that all of these things are essential for students, but none of them showed up in the headlines and many of them are hard to talk with friends about in the course of a normal conversation.

He encouraged both moms to continue to show others the pictures of learning that they often get from their child's classroom. He said the pictures show that something unique is going on. He said he knows people at many of the other schools in the area, and they are studying and learning from their school.

This conversation left Ronny almost excited for the next gathering of her high school friends. It allowed her to remember that comparing schools is truly an apples-to-oranges experiment with each school having its unique signature that provides amazing opportunities for the specific students in their building.

Summary

Apples-to-apples comparison of schools is a very difficult task for parents. Though comparison can be important and helpful in choosing the right school, it can create anxiety about the performance of any individual school. There isn't a best school. Every school looks up to another school as a place that it wished it was more like, so consider focusing on progress. This looks like having more students engaged with their learning. This looks like improvements to the physical space. This looks like new, fresh, and modern ways of teaching including the use of technology tools. It can be hard to believe in the process and growth journey of a school as you hear from others about their schools. We are trapped in a world where social media and most conversations paint the rosiest picture of everything all of the time, and it is important as parent partners to slow judgment, see improvement, and share the good news as it emerges to all that will listen.

9

Having a Plan B

What Can We Do When Our Schools Make Mistakes?

You may not control all the events that happen to you, but you can decide not to be reduced by them.
- Maya Angelou

Seek Positive Solutions for Difficult Situations with Grace

There isn't a parent we have encountered who doesn't want what is best for their child. Every parent has a vision for their child's future, and every parent wants their child to accomplish more than they did. However, sometimes there are barriers to our child's progress that we can't overcome, despite our best efforts. Those barriers can look like anything from a failing grade to a pre-designated class schedule that doesn't allow your child to grow.

School is familiar. Parents understand how students flow through the system, who is in charge, and what the "big picture" looks like. Parents understand how the system works, but mostly from the student's perspective. There exists though, a different playbook for parents that is hyper-dependent upon communication from both the school and our children. We expect that the adults in schools will care for our children as if they were their own and make decisions in their best interests. There are times when that just doesn't happen and information gets "lost in translation." As parents, we have to receive and decode the stories our children tell about school as some are real and some imagined, with the truth lying in between. Understanding that our children don't tell us everything, parents must be vigilant seekers of information. Operating with the belief that "knowledge is power," we should ask questions because understanding the answer supports our ability to make better decisions.

We sometimes make false assumptions that schools don't want to see every student succeed and that they stereotype based on reputation, race, gender, or religion. These false assumptions often arise because of the mistakes that schools do make. When these mistakes occur, we need to be prepared to challenge authority and systems to guarantee our children are recipients of the best possible education. Being well versed in the adult side of the system will allow you to work through some of those emotion-filled situations with grace.

Understanding the System

Like many organizations, schools and school systems are structured on a hierarchy. Someone is in charge of someone else who supervises others. Understanding the hierarchy as well as the correct person to whom your questions and concerns can be directed is important. Systems are segmented into departments that specialize in various aspects of the schooling process (transportation, student assignment, finance, curriculum and instruction, etc.) Often times, upset parents believe that calling the superintendent's office will immediately secure the best outcome to their problem; however, this is generally not the case. It is true that a call to the superintendent's office will often incite immediate action, but not necessarily the desired outcome. Depending upon the size of the district, your call will begin a trickle-down effect; the superintendent's office will call the principal's supervisor, the supervisor will call the principal, the principal will call the teacher, and the teacher will call the parent in an attempt to resolve the issue. By honoring the chain of command, and first calling the teacher and then the principal, parents are more likely to be satisfied with the outcome or solution in the end.

Knowing the rules and policies of the classroom, school, and district will also allow you to better discern the magnitude of a perceived complication. What was once allowable and tolerated may now be grounds for suspension. As an example, the famous holiday movie, *A Christmas Story,* depicts a scene where the main character Ralphie and his friend Flick argue over whether a tongue will stick to the frozen flagpole or not. The exchange, which at one time would have been considered playful banter between boys on the playground, could now be considered harassment or bullying because Flick is left outside by his friends with his tongue frozen to the flagpole. By reading the information that teachers and the school send home, parents will better understand expectations. Our children will make mistakes, but knowing the rules of the game allows parents to better gauge whether the discipline or grading procedures were implemented in a fair and equitable way.

As with any system, there are also unwritten rules to success, many of which can be attributed to the positive relationships between the parent and the school. No matter your ability to be present in the classroom, volunteer for events, or send in supplies, letting the teacher know that there is an inherent level of trust you have in him or her will go far. School staff spend more waking hours with our children than do parents on many days. Demonstrating a genuine interest to the teacher in the work your child does and communicating in a kind and respectful way will send an informal message of trust to those who work most closely with your child.

Bringing a perceived injustice or inadequacy to the attention of school people is hard. The delicate balance between trusting and questioning is one that is best handled by being prepared and emotionally ready for what lies ahead. Considering the following steps may allow a potentially volatile interaction to transpire peacefully.

- OUTLINE YOUR CONCERNS: Be specific when communicating with school personnel about a problem. Identify why you believe there is an issue and connect the concern to the school or district policy that you believe is not being followed. Know that there is a process and you may have to tell your story more than once. Outlining your concern will allow you to be consistent as you work your way up the chain of command.
- GATHER EXAMPLES: Be prepared to back up what you are saying with data. Place documents that illustrate your concern in order and know how each document connects to the issue at hand. Student work samples, report cards, computer generated report updates, screenshots of text messages or pictures, and copies of e-mails are all examples that can be gathered and presented to support your concern. If needed, use sticky notes to jot information down on each artifact to help you remember your thoughts and its connection to the big picture.
- STICK TO THE FACTS: Confronting an issue at the school can be a catalyst for a flurry of emotions. Additionally, there are likely emotions already in play as you are advocating for your child. When engaging school personnel, it is important that you remain in control of your emotions. Taking an extra two or three minutes to breathe deeply and review your notes before entering the school will help you leave the emotional aspects of confrontation behind. Sticking to the facts will also allow you to tell a consistent story as many times as necessary.
- KNOW YOUR EXPECTED OUTCOME: Once you've gathered your data and mentally prepared yourself for the meeting ahead, be sure you know what you expect to occur. Do you want a disciplinary action altered? Do you want your child to have another opportunity to take a test? Do you want the school to communicate better with you so you are better able to partner for your child's success? Be certain to frame your meeting by starting with the end in mind. Articulate that to the people present and let them know the end goal. Although compromise may

be necessary, being sure of the solution or action you are seeking will allow the conversation to remain focused and not be derailed.

The ideas above provide a general framework for parents to enter conversations with the school. To prepare for these crucial conversations, also consider the items below. Many of these have been shown to be effective for other parents, and they may support a productive partnership between home and school.

Write It Out

Take control of any conversation by first writing down all the points you want to cover. Expect there will likely need to be a time for others to respond to each of the points you want to cover. As they talk, take notes so you are prepared to respond. Respond to your notes once the floor is yours.

Help Everyone Understand the Impact

Before you begin your conversation, be clear about how the situation is affecting your child. Is there an issue with an unfavorable decision or is your child upset with an expectation? Is it related to an assignment? Is it about a peer or a friendship? Is there a lack of communication or follow through? All of these can be important reasons to bring an issue to the table, but be able to clearly articulate the impact on your child as well as your family.

Make Appointments

You want to be able to have the full attention of folks when you are communicating about your child. Therefore, it is important to make an appointment to talk with the teacher, counselor, or principal. Requesting an appointment demonstrates a respect for their time but also shows that you are serious enough about the issue to ask for a commitment of their time and yours. Storming into a classroom or office causes an interaction to be unnecessarily defensive, and you may end up leaving more frustrated than when you started because there is not adequate time to devote to resolving your issue.

Keep It Cool

Regardless of how upset or angry you are about your issue, there is little good that will come from raising your voice or cursing. Stay cool, stick to the facts, refer to your notes, and use a tone that demonstrates control over yourself and the situation. Should you begin to waver and emotions are on the brink of bubbling over, consider jotting down notes about what folks are saying so you are able to appear fully present. Use your notes as a support to help you not interrupt and to appear poised and prepared. A person who presents as calm and collected is received much better than a person who begins a conversation irrationally.

Know Your Next Steps

Know, before you enter the meeting or conversation, what your next steps will be if you can't find a satisfactory solution. That is, if you don't leave a conversation with a teacher with a path to a solution, you know to elevate the issue to the principal. Thank the person for their time and confirm who the next person with whom you should speak is. This will send an informal message that you are not satisfied and will continue to seek assistance for your child.

Other Considerations

Working in education is a very demanding profession. The stereotype of teaching being an 8 a.m. to 3 p.m. job with summers off is simply untrue. Most educators work tirelessly to prepare high quality, engaging lessons. They attend training to ensure they stay current on the latest research on effective teaching and learning, and they care deeply for the children with whom they work. Even the best teachers may miss a sign that your child doesn't understand the lesson or was offended by a comment made during class. Approaching things with the assumption that the teacher or principal could be unaware of the situation will allow for a more amicable discussion that will likely lead to both an improved relationship with the school as well as a solution.

Like with most things in life, age brings experience and wisdom. Young teachers enter the profession with the technical knowledge of effective pedagogy and the stages of child development, but experience helps them to grow. They learn the difference between a good lesson and a great lesson; they learn that no two children are the same, and they learn that earning respect is an essential step to their success. Age also can bring the wisdom that comes with parenthood. Becoming a parent as a teacher, unlocks a new level of empathy and concern for the children in their classes.

As with every profession, there are some who excel at the trade and those who struggle with success. Let's be honest, there are teachers who aren't effective. There are even a few who are counting days to retirement. We have to work in partnership to not allow one ineffective teacher to represent the entire grade, school, or profession.

There is no one who cares more about your child than you do. Trust your instinct. If something feels off, investigate. Do not be afraid to ask questions, probe for understanding, and hold folks accountable. There is no one who will advocate with the same passion and determination for quality and equity as you.

There is no one who will fault you for trying to do what is best for your child, but choose your battles. Remember that people are fallible and make mistakes. Determine if the issue is one that, if left alone, will resolve itself. The parent who finds fault with everything that is happening at the school drives a wedge into the parent-school partnership. Building resiliency and experiencing failure are as important to building a strong young adult as is a report card filled with A grades. Your child will have something at school that doesn't go exactly as you feel it should. Equip your child with the skills they need to try to solve their own problems, when appropriate, before you intervene.

PLAN B: A CASE STUDY

The school year had begun and Katrina became more and more difficult to wake each morning. The child, who had always bounded out of her room with a smile, was unusually sullen lately. Conversations over dinner about Katrina's favorite parts of her day were reduced to one or two word answers; "PE," "lunch," and "nothing" were common responses as of late. Cindy had first attributed the change in behavior to Katrina just getting older, however, as she watched and saw that her unhappiness seemed to circle around school, she became more concerned. School had always been a place where Katrina thrived. Since Cindy had received no calls from the school about Katrina, she assumed everything was ok.

One afternoon, Katrina came home from school in tears. Immediately alarmed, Cindy asked Katrina what happened. Katrina told her mother that during class she asked to go to the bathroom, and the teacher refused to allow her to go even when she told her it was an emergency. Katrina said, "Mr. Pfeiffer said I was out of bathroom passes for the week." Cindy then noticed that Katrina was wearing different clothes. She became enraged. As Katrina showered, Cindy opened her Facebook app and scrolled through her feed. Growing increasingly angry because she had not received a call from the school about the matter, coupled with the anxiety she felt because of Katrina's change in behavior toward school, she posted the following: "SO ANGRY! Now I know why my kid hates school! I would too if my trips to the bathroom were limited by tickets! Clearly these people don't understand teenage girls!!!" Living in such a tight knit community, Cindy's post exploded. Posts of support for Katrina as well as negative comments about Katrina's teacher filled her screen. Before she could even consider the impact of her post, Cindy's phone rang. She wasn't surprised to hear the voice of her childhood best friend (who also happened to be the Superintendent's wife) Amy on the other end of the line. Amy always called at just the right time.

After recounting the incident from the day, Cindy told Amy that she was glad she called and hung up the phone feeling more relaxed as she tried to determine the best way to handle all that was happening with Katrina. As the night drew to a close, Cindy and Katrina identified strategies to handle the day ahead and a quiet peace fell within the house. As Cindy and Katrina chatted about the weekend ahead, Cindy's phone rang. Amy's number flashed on the screen and Cindy answered, but Amy wasn't on the line, instead, she heard the voice of Dr. Bellstone, Amy's husband and the superintendent of schools.

Cindy greeted Andrew kindly, but felt a knot growing in her stomach as she knew the reason behind his call. Just a few minutes before the call, Cindy saw that her post from earlier had received a great deal more attention than she anticipated and had thought to herself that after Katrina went to her room she'd remove the post. Cindy now knew that it was too late. Andrew told Cindy that Amy had told him what happened at school and told her he would "take care of it" first thing tomorrow. Cindy didn't know what "take care of it" meant, but something told her there was more trouble facing her ahead.

The following day, Cindy and Katrina reviewed their discussion from the night before and Katrina left for school in a much better mood than Cindy had seen lately. Mid-morning, the phone at Cindy's desk rang. It was Mrs. Dawson, the school principal. She asked Cindy to please come in to see her as soon as she could. Cindy closed up her project and headed to the school.

Mrs. Dawson thanked Cindy for coming and invited her into her office. Once there, Mrs. Dawson began, "Mrs. Cline, this morning I received a rather heated call from Dr. Bellstone asking for details about how the situation with Katrina had been handled. He explained that your Facebook post had been brought to his attention last night, and he was quite concerned that there appeared to be no action from the school. Could you please tell me what he's talking about?"

Cindy felt awful. She knew that Mrs. Dawson's call was at least part of how Dr. Bellstone was "taking care of it." Cindy retold the story from the previous day to Mrs. Dawson. Mrs. Dawson thanked Cindy for the information and shared that she would look into the situation and call her back later that evening. As she walked Cindy to the door, she said, "and please, next time you have a concern, please give me an opportunity to assist you first. Although sharing the information with Dr. Bellstone is certainly appropriate, when you go straight to him it appears as if we aren't trying to make the school a safe and welcoming place for students. Had I known about this incident, I would have certainly spoken with Mr. Pfeiffer before now to get to the bottom of this." She told Cindy that she'd be talking with Katrina but to rest assured this was going to be investigated.

Cindy was exhausted from the day, but knew talking with Katrina was a must for that evening. However, when Katrina came home she burst through the doors in tears and ran past Cindy screaming, "I hate you Mom! Because of your stupid Facebook post the whole school knows what happened yesterday, and Mr. Pfeiffer was a jerk to me today!" Cindy put her head in her hands, wishing she had better controlled her anger, knowing she had another long night ahead.

Morning came and Cindy and Katrina greeted each other as they prepared their lunches for the day. "Good morning Sweetie," Cindy said to Katrina, who coldly replied, "Good morning." Having spent most of the night thinking about the situation Cindy said, "Katrina, I know you are angry, and I'm sorry I hurt you. My post was honest and personal. I should have called Mr. Pfeiffer or Mrs. Dawson instead. I would never intentionally do anything to hurt you." Katrina's back had been to Cindy as she talked, but she heard her voice cracking with emotion and turned to see Cindy's eyes welling with tears. She crossed the room to hug her mother, which allowed the anger of the moment to disappear.

Summary

When we feel that our child is being treated unfairly, it is natural for defense mechanisms to kick in. Understanding the root of the situation, having examples to illustrate your concern, and maintaining control of your emotions will allow you to be well prepared, and move forward toward a solution. As with any relationship, there are good times and stressed times. It is ultimately environment that determines the outcome, and when the environment has mutual trust and respect, a solution is rarely that far away. Be as objective as possible, seek to understand, and forgive when necessary. Provide your child with a positive role model for solving problems and help them understand that all adults make mistakes but with kindness and grace, most can be resolved.

10

Dreaming Big

How Can Sharing Your Family Dreams Support School Partnerships?

We do not fear the unknown:

We fear what we think we know about the unknown.
- Teal Swan

Dreaming for Happiness

Educators should work hard to understand our families and how they dream about happiness. Happiness doesn't have a universal definition, and it is naive to believe that all families have the same hopes and dreams. Having a greater understanding allows us to use our resources, voices, and influence to make this a reality.

Hoping and dreaming isn't enough to bring happiness because there are systems, big and small, intentional and unintentional, that begin to steal hope and stall dreams. Parents rarely see educators fight for the "right" class list and the "right" sections to teach. Parents aren't aware of the ways that some educators create space between themselves and students using the hidden language of the discipline code.

There are secrets in education. Some of them are for survival. Some of them are habits. Some of them are passed down as tricks of the trade. They can include positive strategies like teachers delivering the tough news wedged between two pieces of positive news. They can also include deflating moments like writing up a student on Friday morning because you know that it will impact their weekend or holding a student for a few extra minutes to force them to the end of lunch line.

None of these things in isolation matter to a great degree, but as they add up from kindergarten to graduation, they create friction in the system. All of them can cause death by one thousand cuts to the children and families that need our partnership the most. It is time to bring these things to the surface, so we are working together from the same playbook on crafting the dreams of students.

Speak the Truth of Your Dreams

Schools should fight for dreams, the dreams and vision that families have for their child's future. When students or families talk about how they want to be the first in their family to graduate college, educators need to listen. When a family talks about being dedicated to everyday attendance even with tons of barriers, schools need to truly listen. When the dream of getting a college athletic scholarship is articulated, coaches and communities need to listen with intention. Powerful parent partnerships are forged when the stories around hopes and dreams are unearthed, and they promote a collective hope around student success. Try these tips to begin to forge a collective understanding between parents and the learning community.

- LET LEADERS KNOW ABOUT YOUR FUTURE DREAMS: Often times students will talk about their dreams and hopes with their trusted teachers, but as a parent, it can be incredibly helpful to express those dreams to the building leadership as well.
- DREAM ABOUT SMALL THINGS TOO: Everyone wants to partner around the big dreams, but the small dreams add up to fulfilling hopes as well. Dreaming for your student to enjoy science next quarter matters.
- USE THE PARENT CONFERENCES AS A DREAM SETTING MOMENT: Parent meetings can often devolve into

conversations about solving little issues, but it is important for parents to use this time to talk about dreams and hopes as well.

- DREAM IN COLOR: As families talk about their hopes and dreams with educators, try to be as specific as possible. We want our son to be in the army is different than we imagine our son serving our country and being stationed around the world. Details make dreams come to life.

Beginning to use these tips may feel a bit awkward at first. For many, talking publicly about hopes and dreams can feel like bragging or an opportunity for others to judge you as a parent or family. Most often though, these tips are a fresh opening to a deep line of communication between home and school. Parents who have used these tips continue to get positive feedback and a greater feeling of partnership from the school. Partnering around the dreams of students and families leads to a more personal approach to learning. Here are some other simple, yet powerful, things that parents can do to build a dream team for their child.

Base Dreams on Passions

What does your child love? How could they grow that love and use this interest to serve others?

Talk to Others about Their Dreams

The concept of hopes and dreams can sometimes get lost in the urgent conversations of the day. What did other family members dream about? What are other families at school dreaming about? What do the teachers at the school dream about for their lives? Sharing our dreams with others helps form positive connections and momentum.

See the Dreams in Action

Begin by breaking the larger dreams down into smaller chunks that can be realized. If the dream is to travel, begin by traveling to the next largest city. If the dream is to attend college, schedule a tour of a local university. If the dream is to own a business, visit, support, and connect with business owners.

Make Celebrating Hard Work a Habit

Dreams are often based on a set of successful moments resulting from hard work and perseverance. Identify the small steps that are milestones on the path to the dream. Making this series of events a reality can be challenging and exhausting. It is essential to celebrate on the road to the big dream to keep the emotional tank filled for the journey.

Write Down the Big Dreams

Seeing is believing goes beyond the saying itself. If a family is pursuing dreams, they should have them written down and posted, so that there is a focus, awareness, and reminder all in one place.

Other Considerations

Dreams for our children extend beyond plans after high school. They can and should extend into the type of citizens and human beings we hope to see emerge. What dreams do we have for our children in these spaces?

One hope that is emerging from powerful parent partnerships is how to support the growth of compassion as a dream for our kids. To begin this path, it will require that we surround kids with opportunities to practice, hear stories of, and reflect upon compassion. This dream is miles away for most schools. As we partner on hopes and dreams, we can't forget that compassion is an essential ingredient to making this possible.

Along with feeling compassion, our kids need to see what is possible. Seeing what is possible means an opportunity to be introduced to individuals that mirror their story and have found genuine success and happiness by living out their dreams. Seeing beyond the current reality keeps things in perspective. Life deals hands full of hard moments. For some kids, they will never even understand how hard it can be while others know the pain of making it through each day. We want all students to believe that there is fairness, truth, and justice even though it may not be a part of their current reality.

DREAMING BIG: A CASE STUDY

Living three doors down from the school has its advantages. There are fields and playgrounds. There is no riding the school bus. There are even times when you can stop by school events for a few minutes with no hassle. This is the reality for the Peterson family. A few generations ago, the Peterson family owned all of the property where the school now resides, but today the Peterson home, a three bedroom house, is on a small plot of land occupied by Mr. Peterson, a single dad, his two children and his nephew.

Mr. Peterson knows many of the teachers at the school, especially the veteran teachers. They had been his teachers, and at times, his nemesis as he tried to survive the school day. Daryl Peterson feels like a little boy each time he walks through the door, and this makes him resist each time he is called there for one of his boys.

Daryl has a 10 year old, Peter and an 11 year old, Rianne. Both of his kids struggle at times in school. Their struggles are somewhat linked to attendance, but at times, there are academic and behavioral issues as well. Daryl gets calls about his kids a few times each month. About six months ago, he took on the responsibility of raising his nephew as well. Seven-year-old Malick was born to Daryl's sister who raised him as single mother, but when she lost her fight with cancer, Daryl became Malick's official guardian.

Malick has struggled with school. Some of his troubles appear to be as a result of a learning disability, while other issues appear to be related to the grief and loss of his mother. Daryl knew that his children would be a great support to their cousin, but he also knew that Malick and school may be a difficult mix. Daryl felt like he was a supportive dad. He talked to his kids about finishing their homework. He got them up for school each morning, and he provided some rewards for grades and good behavior.

Apparently this wasn't enough. Daryl was getting calls each week about Malick and the other two children. The amount of stress that school created for him was growing. As the second half of the year began, Daryl was called to the principal's office. His anxiety was at an all-time high as he worried about the future of his children.

As the meeting began, Daryl soon realized that this visit was different. The principal, who many years ago had played football with Daryl's younger brother, asked Daryl a set of questions that he hadn't thought about or considered in a long time. Mr. Arrington asked about Daryl's dreams for the kids. What would make him a proud father? What does future happiness look like for the kids? What dreams could they start working on together?

Following that meeting, Daryl was able to feel a different connection to the school. He was able to forget, just for a moment, how this building and many of its teachers had impacted him. He was also able to think forward and consider that all of his kids, including his struggling nephew Malick, had dreams that he and the school could support together.

This meeting and those questions didn't fix everything, but it did help. Daryl still got calls about behavior and attendance, but they were coupled with comments about the dreams that everyone knew they were pursuing together. Peter wanted to work with his hands fixing things, so they were finding ways to make that happen by helping him select classes that would put him in line for an apprenticeship his junior year. Rianne wanted to pursue fashion design, so at home they supported her dreams by buying a great drawing notebook and a full length mirror. Malick wanted to be an American Ninja Warrior (yes some of our dreams fit into unique categories) so the school and Daryl found a way to get him to the rock climbing gym across town for some free lessons.

Together families and schools have an opportunity to forge powerful small moments that can accelerate dreams and open the doors to what is truly possible.

Summary

As we ask parents and schools to dream big for kids, it is important that we also remember that we need to dream big about how our system can support this work. The speed of life isn't slowing down, and its impacts continue to hit all families, especially those with the most need. This is putting pressure on schools to change. It is urgent that we continue to fix our systems from the inside so as not to let the erosion of trust from the outside eat it away. Parents and educators, in partnership, can't support everything that exists in the current system and then hope that the dreams of our kids will be fulfilled. We need to ask the adults in our school system to think differently and act differently. Modern schools that support the dreams of families realize that communities are assets. They focus on bringing the community into the school, and they reach out for community partners because they realize that, together, the solutions are more rich and robust.

In addition, the schools that we look to support with powerful parent partnerships seek new ways to solve old problems, spend time listening to and knowing each other's stories, celebrate life together, communicate around the hard stuff as opposed to avoiding it, and ask for forgiveness when they screw up.

It is great to dream about these types of schools. These are the schools with a culture that supports healthy kids. These are the schools that understand that their mission is complex. These are the types of schools where emotions like joy, fun, and excitement are real and genuine, and these are the schools where dreams grow and kids are truly successful.

11

Sharing the Excellent Part of the School

A Successful School has a Compelling Story on How it Supports Learning

Great stories happen to those who can tell them.
- Ira Glass

Stories are Central

From the beginning, parents are telling stories. They are picking up books and reading them to their children. They are passing along oral history. They are telling amazing tales to help children fall asleep, but soon they are sharing these storytelling duties with the facilitators of learning in schools. Students are then surrounded by constant story. It shapes their understanding and allows them to make sense of their complex world.

Stories begin to shape what is seen as good and right, and they illuminate the things that weigh us down. It is story that can bring us happiness in sad moments, and it is story that can bring perspective to confusing moments. Stories are the evidence that allows us to make judgments about what serves us well and what does not, and it is the stories about schools that allow communities to build a narrative about the effectiveness of education.

Stories about schools paint a picture about what learning should look like, and stories about schools help us understand the learning experience of students. Stories connect past learning models to future possibilities in learning, and stories provide parents with the information they need to share to the greater community about how schools serve their students. Stories are powerful.

Stories are a powerful weapon as well. If we share the stories that showcase the humanity of children in their worst moments, people begin to believe that these stories represent the totality of the culture of a school. If we share the stories of pain, tension, and stress that are a natural part of a learning organization, there are many that see this from a deficit mindset. Stories without context, stories without perspective, and stories embedded in the wrong emotions can fracture the potential for a powerful parent partnership.

Stories are central to the work. Stories can cultivate success. Stories are what keeps us from the shifts in mindset that we need.

Being a Powerful Storyteller

Students tell us stories about school each day. They tell us about the amazing experiment in science class, and they also share how "boring" and "dumb" school can be. All of these stories hold pieces of truth. Some of which we share with others, and other pieces we store for later or choose just to discard as silliness. Schools send parents pieces of the story as well. E-mails, newsletters, and phone calls all make up a web of information that, cobbled together, becomes the narrative of the school. Other parents, community members, and alumni share pieces of the story as well. Each of these inputs are part of the 1000-piece puzzle that makes up the truth about how a school serves its students, families and community.

There is an increasing pressure on schools to tell their story. The media coverage of schools tends to focus on the negative moments as they lead to more clicks, more viewers, and more traffic in the comments section. Unfortunately, this puts schools and districts under greater pressure to paint an accurate picture about the amazing work happening inside the walls of the school. Doing this well requires empowering both parents and students to be storytellers. Parents are taking on this role of champion and ambassador for their schools because they want more people in the community and beyond to have an accurate picture of the short- and long-term successes that are happening. If you choose to embrace these roles as a parent partner, try these tips to begin:

- ASK ABOUT THE LEARNING: School leaders often feel like they are conveying the vision and mission of what takes place at the school. This initial message from the principal can sound like a fluffy sound bite, but the story of learning at the school goes beyond that. Ask the principal for the 2–3 minute or longer version.
- TALK ABOUT THE NEAT STUFF: Every school is doing some things that bring fun and joy to learning. It is important that we share these moments. There is plenty of time to be serious about learning, but let's make sure to tell the stories of kids enjoying their time at school.
- TALK ABOUT THE NECESSARY STUFF: Schools are supporting all of the needs of children better than ever. Make sure to share the stories of the counselors, social workers, food bank, health services, and the other necessary services that really make a school tick.
- FOCUS ON COMMUNITY: Schools are an essential part of an excellent community. Schools serve the community in a variety of ways. They play the role of community center, and the students often complete hours of community service. All of these are ripe for stories to share with others.
- READ ABOUT STORYTELLING AND SCHOOLS: There are a number of amazing books about how schools use story to build capacity. Consider reading *Storycatchers* by Christina Baldwin or *BrandED* by Eric Sheninger and Trish Rubin.

Beginning as School Ambassador

After learning about more of the stories that surround the school, parents can begin to share an accurate picture of the school. Learning communities need parents and others willing to take time to share the current success stories. They also need folks to talk about the future learning opportunities that kids will have to neighbors, colleagues, and friends. Consider these steps as you begin this journey.

Share Less about Test Scores and More about Excellence

In a narrative dominated by test scores, powerful parent partners can have a tremendous impact on how a school is viewed by focusing on the excellence happening on a day-to-day basis. The achievement of students is essential, but it is a byproduct of small moments of excellence happening throughout a school community. Tell these stories to those that will listen that these are the essential aspects of an excellent modern school.

Share Less about Individual Students and More about the Collective Feel of the School

The individual stories about students misbehaving or doing things out of the ordinary can quickly be viewed as the norm when that isn't the reality. The community can begin to believe that many or all of the students are like this, but the best ambassadors are able to tell the story about the positive energy in the building and how pleasant it is to be at the school. They also tell the "boring" story about how every time they go into the school, they are amazed at the number of students who are on-task and working hard.

Share Fewer Weaknesses and More Strengths

It is human nature to notice issues, problems, and struggles. This fact can lead us to comments and conversations about these things throughout the day. As champions for schools, it is important to push back against this and shape our conversations around the strengths. This doesn't mean making things up, and it doesn't mean stretching the truth. It means being intentional to accentuate the positive, repeat the excellent moments to multiple audiences, and continue to showcase the strengths of the school.

Showcase Modern Learning

There are three areas that all schools are pursuing in order to prepare students to be excellent citizens and solution makers. These include: issuing technology as a tool to support all subjects of learning, creating learning experiences that feature projects to showcase understanding, and using the community to bring context and meaning to learning. As a champion, ambassador, and parent, you don't have to understand all of the details around these efforts, but it is helpful to share that these are key reasons why students enjoy their experiences and reasons why you support and promote the school.

Work with Your School to Develop an "Elevator Speech"

The public's perception about a school is often based on the stories told. Be intentional. Work with school-based leadership teams to develop a personal "two-minute" elevator speech about the school, and then share the message as a consistent response to questions about your school.

Other Considerations

As parents embrace this role, they often wonder what questions they should be asking of the principal, teachers, and others working in the building. Here are four great questions that can unearth accurate information that can be shared into the community. What should I be telling my neighbors? What stories should be told more often? Where will we be in five years? What partnerships make us great? Each of these questions allows school leaders to unpack educational jargon as well as showcase the heart and compassion of an organization.

Parents who are school partners can also support another key aspect of telling the story of a school, the non-verbals of a school. Many visitors and community members form their impressions of a school based on the outdoor signage, the grounds of the building, and the entryway. Supporting beautification efforts, redesigning common spaces, and keeping signage updated are all small things that have big impact on telling the story of the school.

One final idea about how to support the school surrounds how to interrupt stories that paint an inaccurate picture of the school. Most parents have been in a situation when a fellow parent or community member is commenting on the school and it is clear that they don't have all of the information or inaccurate information. It is an awkward moment. As a parent, you may want to say something, but you aren't sure what to say. You know that the comments are painting the wrong picture of the school, and you know that others will get the wrong impression, but you don't know what to say. In those moments, we suggest trying the following replies:

- Have you asked the teacher or principal about what happened? I bet they know the whole story and will share as much as possible.
- That seems odd. That's not been my experience with the school.
- What do you think that we can do to help with that?

PAINTING A TRUE PICTURE: A CASE STUDY

Hannah was upset. Her son Larry had experienced something at school that was awful. Anti-Semitic remarks were directed toward Larry by another student. The remarks left the student mad and confused, and it left the family angry. The mother turned this anger to her popular community blog.

Hannah posted a message on social media explaining that her son was a victim of these remarks at school, and that she was disappointed and angry that children should have to hear these things. This message elicited 75 reactions and 22 comments over the next six hours. Comments included things like, "I can't believe that the school allows things like this to happen"; "I wouldn't let my daughter go to a school where that happened"; "You should call the news station. This is outrageous."

The next morning, the school principal, during student drop off, had a parent stop for an extra few seconds to say, "I'm sorry about what happened with Larry. I know that you work hard to keep things like that from happening at our school." The principal thanked the parent, finished student drop off, and returned to his office. He had no idea what the parent was talking about, but there were only two students named Larry, so he could figure it out.

He asked a few teachers and his assistant. They didn't know what had happened. He would guess which family to call first. Luckily he guessed right. The principal mentioned that he had heard from another parent that Larry may have had an issue at school yesterday (not knowing if it was the right family). Larry's Mom said that she was planning to call later in the day, but she assumed that he already knew what had happened.

Hannah told the principal about the comments. The principal showed empathy for the family, outlined next steps, and within the hour had the two students involved in a restorative practice with the social worker. Unfortunately, the damage had been done. Hundreds of individuals had a data point about the school culture, the way that the school handles things, and a sense of the type of school that Larry attends.

It is in these moments that school leaders often struggle because, if given an opportunity to solve an issue in a timely way, they would have showcased the incredible work of the school to support students and create an amazing environment for learning. The 24-hour news cycle and social media can make this a difficult facet of an already difficult role of being a school leader.

About a week later, the principal had marked on his calendar to circle back with the family to see how things were going. He called Larry's mother, and she thanked him for his support and reported that things were going well for Larry. She even mentioned that Larry and the other student were potentially on the road to being friends.

The principal asked near the end of the conversation for a favor. He explained how being a principal in an era of social media is very difficult, and how he tries to be responsive to every incident that he knows about. He talked about how quickly the perception of a school can shift in a community based on one or two stories that spread without all of the details. He wanted to figure out a way to help all parents understand how they can support the school by sharing the amazing things of the school, and he was also looking for strategies to help parents pause before posting when there was an issue, so the school had a chance to react.

This was a complex conversation. He didn't want to accuse Hannah of doing the wrong thing with her post. He wasn't trying to mute her free speech, but he was asking for a partnership that could help the school grow and expand the knowledge of the community about the opportunities at the school. The principal knows that he needs the voice of all of the parents to build a true picture of what happens inside the school. He also knows that one story, one moment, one piece of half information shared with the wrong audience can derail a lot of hard work and progress. He was glad that the parent accepted his invitation to work on this together.

Summary

Schools need to not only tell their story, but sell their story as well. It isn't about creating something that isn't true, but it is shaping the beauty, assets, and strengths into a coherent message that resonates with everyone in the ecosystem. Schools are trying to tell these stories in a very noisy time. There is information everywhere, but rarely is it stitched together into a coherent message.

More and more school leaders are looking for parents to share this message and story. They are documenting the modern learning that is happening, and they are articulating the amazing experiences that occur within the walls of the school. The time has come to amplify this message, and it will take parent partners to make this a reality as it takes time for the greater community to hear, believe, and act on the message.

Story is powerful, and it will be the lever of change that transforms many schools into the places of learning that everyone envisions. Story is the way that we can reach the head and the heart, and story is what allows us to care for each other in tough moments and celebrate together in the best moments.

Conclusion

Today many of our schools still engage families in traditional ways. Only recently have we seen a shift in the partnership philosophy between school and home that recognizes the need to engage in a common support of kids. This looks like parents truly understanding why specific teaching and learning dictates their child's success. It looks like conferences led by students who allow their voice and expertise to shine. It feels like schools and families together challenging the status quo to push the boundaries. These are the new powerful parent, family and school partnerships. This isn't the reality in most schools though, and this book has outlined many ways to begin the shift.

Research around parent involvement is clear. It tells us that "students with parents who are involved in their school tend to have fewer behavioral problems and better academic performance, and are more likely to complete high school than students whose parents are not involved in their school."[1] With so many things competing for our time and attention, it is more important, now than ever, that we maintain an interest in our children's school experiences from the time they enter school until graduation as "parental involvement in school correlates to higher grade point averages."[2]

Moving from the current model that yields the same results means acknowledging that much is broken in the modern parent partnership. It lacks the ability to leverage change and nurture the modern school. Principals, parents, and all that surround schools should begin today to engage in new conversations around the topics throughout the book and the questions below that can serve as a starting point for paving a new road to powerful parent partnership.

How Can I Keep from Being Surprised by my Child's Grades?

In too many places, grades are the binder for parent partnerships. The quarterly report card, online grade notifications, and the papers that come home with grades are the core of the partnership. This has the potential for wrong and misleading information to be at the core of the conversation. Parents need to be careful about using every grade and all of the points entered into the gradebook as their reality about learning and progress. Teachers and leaders need to know that a parent needs context around grades that can help their conversations at home. In order to keep from grades being the central tenet of the partnership and most importantly making sure that grades aren't a surprise, schools need to talk about grades more holistically and focus on the importance of learning over the collection of points. Schools and parents need to agree that shifts in learning behaviors (not turning in assignments, doing poorly on assessments, having holes in their learning) require an activation of all parts of the school/family partnership, and that the report card should only be a final document outlining what has been known by all parties (students, parents, teachers, and leaders) throughout the learning segment (quarter, semester, etc.)

Why Should I Come to Teacher Conferences?

As Sherri Wilson, former senior manager of family engagement at the National Parent Teacher Association, says, "The most important way for family members to get involved is to show interest in the student's academics at home."[3] Engaging face to face with your child's teacher provides a window into the physical space your child visits each day. It allows you an opportunity to see the type of work that is valued and showcased, and provides time for conversations that focus solely on your child and their performance. On the flip side, attending parent-teacher conferences sends an informal message to the teacher and school that you value their work with your child. Parent conferences are one of the few times that folks from home and school are in the same place and are focused on the child. The face-to-face dynamic solidifies the partnership between school and home and opens the door for ongoing, asynchronous communication.

What Can I Do if My Child Doesn't Like the Way the Teacher Teaches?

Inevitably all students will have a teacher with whom they don't connect. Digging to find the root cause of why your child feels disconnected is the first step to resolving this problem. Asking your child questions like, "Is there something specific that your teacher says or does that makes you feel this way?" or, "Can you tell me about a time when you felt that way in class?" These questions will help you to determine if the child's complaint needs to be investigated or if their issue is rooted in the teacher holding them to higher expectations than they have had in the past. Anytime your child expresses concern over being treated unfairly, inequitably, or has ongoing complaints of boredom, you should to talk with the teacher about your concerns to find a mutually agreeable solution. Also, helping your child to understand that in life they will possibly work with folks who they don't particularly like and equipping them with strategies to cope will be a life lesson that will go a long way.

How can Coaches Fit into the Partnership?

Many teachers serve schools in dual roles that interact with students in different ways, their role in covering academic content and the role of sports team coach. The informal relationships that exist between students and their coaches are unique. Characterized by an almost friend-like dynamic, coaches have influence over our children in powerful ways. In school, coaches are required to monitor grades and general academic performance to ensure ongoing eligibility to participate, but the dynamic often has a much greater reach. Coaches talk to their colleagues to find out why students are struggling, act as intermediary, and place high expectations for success on the students with whom they work. Many times, students will do, say, and act in ways purely to have favor with the coach. Families can call upon coaches directly to support their children when their level of influence is paramount to the student's success.

Why does Homework Feel so Different These Days?

Homework has been a wedge in school-family partnerships for many years. Some parents will feel that schools have gone soft without mountains of homework while other parents look to recapture family time that is lost to arguments around homework completion. There are camps of educators who are absolutists. They believe that homework is an essential continuation of learning that can help to thread together family partnerships, while others are staunch advocates for homework-free schools. The answer isn't at the extremes, but it lies in healthy partnership between home and school. This kind of partnership trusts that parents can ask for more time without homework for the sake of the family, extracurricular activities, and self-care, and it is a partnership where the school can ask for some moments at home to be spent in meaningful, relevant work that allows a student's learning space to extend beyond the classroom. The concept of homework is also changing. Students are being asked to collect data, do interviews, gather digital images, and design with digital tools. All of these things can feel foreign to parents. They may not have had these experiences and may struggle to know how to assist. Powerful parent partners support students in these moments with time and space that support thinking, creativity, and hard work. They also ask questions. Is this your best work?

Are you sure that you reviewed the guidelines or rubric? How can I help? Asking questions shows a spirit of partnership and interest, and often, the questions themselves will support the students through the process.

What's My Role as a Parent in My Child's Digital World?

The addition of powerful mobile devices into the hands of younger and younger students has added to the complexity of school/home partnerships. Schools and parents are trying to figure out how much to limit students technology use to allow for more time and attention to meaningful tasks and learning, without limiting the informal learning that occurs in their digital world. There is a fine line between helping kids to learn appropriate use of devices and pushing back against the addictive nature of the social media algorithms that draw kids back to their phones over and over throughout the day. Together, schools and family can have a united message that having all of the information in the world at our fingertips is a powerful learning tool that requires an incredible amount of responsibility. These responsibilities include: making time for face-to-face collaboration, critically deciding the truth from a variety of information, remaining compassionate with online communication, and finding a balance between green time and screen time for the purpose of mental health and wellness. These items need to be essential conversations on both sides of the partnership, so that students hear from different perspectives how the issues around devices go well beyond "put them away" and "you are always on your screen."

How is the Home Language of Your Students Mirrored in Your School?

As our schools continue to welcome more students that are at various levels of learning English, it becomes more important for teachers and leaders to partner with parents and serve students. Language barriers are not necessarily a new challenge in many of our schools, but we would be remiss if we did not mention it. Schools have a variety of ways to extend a hand in partnership to students and families with another language. It can start with ensuring that images in our schools represent all of our families and the many beautiful differences that they bring to the table. Additionally, schools should consider offering paperwork in native languages, sending messages to families via e-mail, text, and voice in their preferred language, and providing interpreters for all school events so families feel welcome. It also means being thoughtful about the school calendar to avoid any conflicts with cultural or religious observances. Partnership means allowing the school to be a safe place, a sanctuary, where families can work to become more comfortable in the community and be free from community and political concerns.

How do We Make Sure Schools are Inclusive of All Types of Families?

The title of this book is *Powerful PARENT Partnerships*, but it is important to remember that the term *parent* is one that can be defined in several ways. It is essential that our schools are welcoming and open to not only the traditional nuclear family, but also to others who are charged with raising children. Parents of all types, those with domestic partners, those who are in single-parent homes, and the extended family members serving as parents, should feel as included as does the president of the PTA. Schools should make certain that the resources teachers use reflect the diverse perspectives of the cultures that are a part of the school community. Each student should be able to see him or herself in the images that are posted around the school and are on display for the public. For true partnerships to exist, thoughtful and dedicated efforts to engaging all parents must be in the core mission and vision of the school.

Is there Value to Perfect Attendance?

Being at school is important. Children are learning how to navigate social situations, collaborate on a deep level, and work through moments of critical thinking facilitated by the teacher. The physical concept of school, done with excellence, isn't going away. In addition, being at school builds a lifelong habit around being reliable and punctual. Attendance is no substitute for life experiences though. If a family has an opportunity to connect with relatives from out of state or country during school, leaders need to see this as learning. If families have an opportunity to travel to experience a new part of the country or where generations past lived, this is learning and often creates experiences and memories that last a lifetime. Attendance and instructional time are seen as sacred, but the evolution of where and how students are learning demands more flexibility. Parents shouldn't be forced to unenroll students if they are gone for a week, and students shouldn't be guilt-ridden because of perverse attendance incentives about missing a day. In a partnership, there is a balance to be struck between the learning and family moments that shape children in amazing ways. This partnership begins with families communicating before planned events, and the school entering into these conversations with an energy of support; both their excitement for the experience and an excitement for the student to return.

Final Thoughts

Though no partnership is perfect, the partnerships described throughout this book have a few things in common. They are deeply focused on kids. They are based in hope that progress and change is possible, and they recognize that many old traditions fail in today's schools. With these commonalities, we can go forward together with this renewed mission for powerful partnerships: partnerships that see families as assets, recognize the hard work needed, and have empathy and compassion as their core; partnerships where schools and families share a common definition of success.

Notes

1 A.T. Henderson and N. Berla (1994), *A new generation of evidence: The family is critical to student achievement*. Washington, DC: National Committee for Citizens in Education.
2 www.sedl.org/connections/resources/evidence.pdf
3 www.usnews.com/education/blogs/high-school-notes/2012/02/20/students-learn-better-with-engaged-parents